How and what would you write to someone who gave birth to you? It's the beautiful premise that threads this heartfelt compendium of letters by sons and daughters addressed to mothers, some living and others who have passed on. On one level, it's an ode to the importance of parental love and the bond which still binds across time and space, even when, no, especially when things get tough. On the other, it's retrospection of a deeper kind, a mirror for self-reflexivity, to really see clearly, warts and all, without any pretence.

YEOW KAI CHAI
Poet and Former Director, Singapore Writers Festival

Here are stories of a-witnessing in so far as the child watches and bears witness to the mother. Some stories will leave you in wonderment and not a little envious. If you were a mother, you might even panic at some. Will you be seen as the mother is seen here? There is no rulebook for mothers, and, if there is one it should best be eschewed. For the most heart-breaking stories are the ones that stick strictly to rules. These letters are most illuminating when they speak to the tenuous link between mother and child aspirations/expectations and reality. It is a privilege to be allowed access to them.

DANA LAM
*Writer/Performer, Still Life (2019),
and Associate Artist with Checkpoint Theatre*

Letter to my Mother

Letter to my Mother

Words of love and perspectives on growing up from sons and daughters

Edited by Felix Cheong

Text © individual contributors as credited in each work
© 2021 Marshall Cavendish International (Asia) Private Limited

Published in 2021 by Marshall Cavendish Editions
An imprint of Marshall Cavendish International

All rights reserved

No part of this publication may be reproduced, stored in a retrieval system or transmitted, in any form or by any means, electronic, mechanical, photocopying, recording or otherwise, without the prior permission of the copyright owner. Requests for permission should be addressed to the Publisher, Marshall Cavendish International (Asia) Private Limited, 1 New Industrial Road, Singapore 536196. Tel: (65) 6213 9300 E-mail: genref@sg.marshallcavendish.com Website: www.marshallcavendish.com

The publisher makes no representation or warranties with respect to the contents of this book, and specifically disclaims any implied warranties or merchantability or fitness for any particular purpose, and shall in no event be liable for any loss of profit or any other commercial damage, including but not limited to special, incidental, consequential, or other damages.

Other Marshall Cavendish Offices:
Marshall Cavendish Corporation, 800 Westchester Ave, Suite N-641, Rye Brook, NY 10573, USA • Marshall Cavendish International (Thailand) Co Ltd, 253 Asoke, 16th Floor, Sukhumvit 21 Road, Klongtoey Nua, Wattana, Bangkok 10110, Thailand • Marshall Cavendish (Malaysia) Sdn Bhd, Times Subang, Lot 46, Subang Hi-Tech Industrial Park, Batu Tiga, 40000 Shah Alam, Selangor Darul Ehsan, Malaysia

Marshall Cavendish is a registered trademark of Times Publishing Limited

National Library Board, Singapore Cataloguing-in-Publication Data

Names: Cheong, Felix, editor.
Title: Letter to my mother: words of love and perspectives on growing up from sons and daughters / edited by Felix Cheong.
Description: Singapore : Marshall Cavendish Editions, [2021]
Identifiers: OCN 1242596168 | ISBN 978-981-4928-77-9
Subjects: LCSH: Children—Correspondence. | Mothers. | Mother and child.
Classification: DDC 306.8743—dc23

Printed in Singapore

Cover design by Adithi Khandadai

This book is dedicated to all parents,
in the hope that these shared experiences will
inspire and shape your own parenting journey.

Contents

Foreword **FELIX CHEONG**	11
Love Without Borders **IRENE NG**	17
When Little Daughters Become Little Women **SHARDA HARRISON**	28
Guilt, Survived **CHERYL CHARLI TAN**	37
I Am My Mother's Son **WILLIAM PHUAN**	44
A Magic Pearl **LYDIA KWA**	54
Dear Jenny **REGINA DE ROZARIO**	64
Thank You, Mummy **ROSE MARIE SIVAM**	72
Joy. Luck. Club **GEORGETTE YU**	79
11 Years **ZURAIDAH MOHAMED**	88
Mother's Mother Tongue **GWEE LI SUI**	98

Don't Hedge Your Bets 108
Wahid Al Mamun

Now and Always 119
Jean Tan

My Mom, My World 129
Jo-Anne Lee

Mama, Live 137
Faith Ng

Rest if You are Tired 144
Martha Tara Lee

Letter to My Mother, Lim Siew Lian Veronica 153
Beverly Morata Grafton

The Battle for My Left Hand 163
Charmaine Deng

A Necessary Detour 172
Nanny Eliana

My Mother and Her Unprintable Life 183
Christine Chia

Letter to My Mother 192
Tania De Rozario

Foreword

Felix Cheong

When was the last time you spoke to your mother? Do you remember the drift of that conversation, its turns and tide, its tone and tales? What would you have edited out if you had recorded it and replayed it as a memory?

I never got round to a last conversation with Mum in her final days. Discharged from Changi General Hospital on Christmas Eve, 2019, she was living on borrowed time, with only one lung doing the work of two. Even hooked up to an oxygen tank, she was gasping, like a diver drowning in fresh air. There was no float she could hold onto to keep her body from sinking into itself.

By then, pneumonia had already widowed her. Dad, her husband of 56 years, died on December 12, barely a fortnight before. And pneumonia would soon orphan my brothers and me on January 3.

How swiftly death comes, and how mute.

Not that Mum had much to say. Her words had already been cut down to size since 2015, when vascular dementia began eating her from the inside out. Words were precious and few, more so now that every breath was a fight to stay awake, stay the execution. Whatever she could manage was guttural, often cries of pain as her diapers was being changed.

When I visited her on New Year's Day, she was pale and weak, weakened still by a lack of appetite. She could barely sit up. Her body was shutting down for the long sleep ahead.

"How are you feeling?" I asked in Cantonese.

"Aaah," Mum said, raspy. "Very pain."

I, the writer-son she had been proud of, who would dedicate his next two books to his late parents, could offer no words of comfort at that point. All the poems I had ever written about death, its long blade and its long wake trailing into the night, were mute. No lyrical flourishes could have explained how her husband had slipped away without one last look; no language came close to breaching the divide between the living and dying.

I sat with Mum for a while, and left soon after. The next time I sat by her side, her face was already cold but not stiff yet. Again, words failed me. I fell back on – and was held up in grace by – the Lord's Prayer, the Hail Mary and the Glory Be.

Borrowed words, but they burrowed deep.

Over the next few weeks, I would be haunted by what I did not manage to say to Mum. All the thanks I could have offered; all the memories I could have told her that I cherish; all the things she had taught me; all the sacrifices she had made to bring us up – and I said nothing.

At the far end of the long corridor of grief, I soon realised, stood regret. I met it, asked to be relieved of the burden but instead, it walked me down another long corridor where guilt awaited.

All I could do was visit Mum's niche, her urn next to Dad's, touch their picture gently and whisper my thanks, over and belatedly, till something broke up, broke down or broke away.

Whatever it was, however it did, almost three months after her passing, I dreamt of Mum:

DREAMING OF MUM

I dreamt of you last night, Mum.
I was piggybacking you, as you must have done with
me once.
The day was dusk but felt like dawn.
The wind was light and so were you,
All spirit and spirited, the weight
Of being dead lifted, like an early Easter.

I was a little hunched, talking, in Cantonese,
A bit of this and a hunch about that, turning inanities
Inside out into a conversation.
It was like old times many times over.
You laughed often - can't remember why -
But it made the trudge uphill eventful.

I never got round to where we were heading.
Wakefulness snatched me
And left me knowing.
It is coming to the end of 100 days

Since you left without saying goodbye.
But this, I know, Mum.

You are now in a better place, as the cliché goes.
This poem is tearing even as it finds its words,
Not from sadness or fear, but a dream-like insight
That you are safe, as free of ash and dust
As my dearest memory of your laugh.

I finally had that last conversation with Mum.

***

In this anthology of 20 letters, our contributors from all walks of life got to write their letter to their mother. To a man, and woman, they all found the task extremely difficult, probably the most painful and private thing they had ever put pen to paper (or fingers to screen). Many confessed afterwards they had to finish writing it in tears (as I did with this foreword).

For some of them, their mother had long passed away, so their letter became a requiem, a way to summon her memory, a callout that she had not been forgotten. For others whose mother is alive and well, their letter was a thank-you card for the years that gratitude had not been expressed in person. And for a handful, their letter was not so much peace talk as a negotiation with their past in which their mother's shadow was writ large.

Above all, *Letter to My Mother* is an honest, raw and emotional read. It is written with much love (and sometimes with its alter ego, hate) and humanity. And hopefully, after

Felix (right) and his mother.

reading these letters, you will ask yourself the questions I had posed you earlier:

When was the last time you spoke to your mother? Do you remember the drift of that conversation, its turns and tide, its tone and tales? What would you have edited out if you had recorded it and replayed it as a memory?

Felix Cheong is the author of 19 books, including six volumes of poetry, a trilogy of satirical flash fiction and five children's picture books. His works have been nominated for the prestigious Frank O'Connor Award and the Singapore Literature Prize. His latest work is a libretto written with composer Chen Zhangyi, *Panic Love: An A Cappella Opera*, released as a music video.

Conferred the Young Artist Award in 2000, Felix holds a Masters in Creative Criting and is currently a university adjunct lecturer with the National University of Singapore, University of Newcastle, Murdoch University and Curtin University.

Love Without Borders

Irene Ng

Dearest Mum,

As I write this, the wind is whipping outside and the rain is spitting. This is pretty normal weather in Scotland. This sort of freezing rain, interspersed with snow and sleet, is not quite what we are used to in the tropics. I am thinking of you, Mum, in the biting cold of a Scottish winter, and thinking too of the distance between us.

It pains me that we have not met for more than a year. The Covid-19 pandemic has all but brought travel to a halt. You are in Penang in lockdown Malaysia, and I am in Hawick in lockdown Scotland, and we cannot meet in Singapore as we used to either, what with the strict quarantine rules.

I am sorry to have been away from home in Penang for so long, getting further and further from you as time goes on.

When you waved goodbye to me the first time I left for Singapore in 1980, did you know that I would be away for good? I was then 16. Singapore, the city of my dreams, beckoned and

I responded, carrying with me only one suitcase onto the night train. Packing had to be pared down to the essentials – clothes, family photos, and school textbooks. Just enough to get me through two years of study at a junior college.

As the train pulled away on that moonlit night, I felt as if I was leaving everything I held dear, but when I looked at your face with your gentle smile, I knew that home still waited for me, that the moon still illuminated the quiet lanes to our house in Bukit Mertajam (BM). The memory of your smile on that wrenching night was sealed and stamped with a timeless love that has stayed with me all these years.

Together with Dad, you made your way to visit me in Singapore several months later. It took about 13 hours overnight on a bus from BM to Singapore, and then on a cab from the bus depot to see me. You found me alone in the corner of some stranger's house, wilting in a rented room in the old, dingy bungalow that smelled of musty mould.

To be honest, I am not sure if I could have endured for much longer if you had not brought your reassuring smile and loving embrace. Also, a fried white pomfret. My favourite type of fish. Then after several treasured hours together, you took the bus back that very evening, another 13 hours on the road with two pit stops. Staying overnight in a hotel room was then not an option.

Those were the days when we had to count every cent. Our family was going through a bad financial patch. We hardly talk about those years. Not because we are ashamed of it, I think, but because we are not the sort to dwell on the difficulties; at least, we became that sort. We just adjusted, together. Living frugally became ingrained.

In any case, it is easier to linger on the happier times, and we had plenty. But I just want to say that it was during those tough days, when it seemed as if the rain would never stop beating down and the wind would never stop howling, that I learnt the most from you, and loved you most. You showed me what unconditional love was really about, and what real strength looked like.

Your courage in letting me leave for Singapore made all the difference in my life. I know it was not an easy decision.

It was not only that I was your only daughter. Or that *Koko* (Elder Brother), five years my senior, was also away, studying in a university in Kuala Lumpur where he now lives. It was also the social and cultural pressures – many tradition-minded relatives asked why I could not make do with studying in Penang, like their daughters did. It would certainly be easier on the purse.

But you chose to give more weight to the words of my convent school teacher. She believed, bless her, that I would have better opportunities to further myself in Singapore. The systemic racial discrimination in Malaysia would hold me back, and hold me down, even if I might be a top student, she thought.

But in truth, no one knew then whether that really counted for anything, or what the future would hold for me in competitive Singapore. I had no friends or relatives there. I had never travelled further than Cameron Highlands, our most exotic holiday to date then. If you feared for me, you never showed it. You allowed me to make my own life, one with wider horizons. For that, I can never thank you enough.

You have lived your entire life in Penang, and until I moved to Singapore, had never ventured out of Malaysia. Raised in a strict Peranakan Chinese household, your parents' dream for you, their only daughter, was to marry a man, preferably rich, and to bear babies, preferably sons. You came from a refined and wealthy background, surrounded by intricate jade jewellery and handcrafted furniture inlaid with mother-of-pearl.

In his heyday, Grandpa, a businessman, cut a distinguished figure in his crisply-starched white shirt, pressed black trousers, and leather shoes, the gleam of which was matched only by his shiny black Morris Minor. And there was Grandma, in her batik sarong and lace *baju kebaya* fastened with her gold *kerongsang* brooch. Everything in their house was orderly, including the pile of *The Straits Times* newspapers stacked in a perfect block.

But your life was anything but orderly. You started school late at 11 because of the Japanese Occupation, and left school early because of marriage. You married Dad, then a teacher, in your early 20s. He might not be rich by Grandpa's standards, but he offered something you needed: Love, stability, and a freedom of sorts. Also, you were awfully keen on ballroom dancing and he proved nifty with his footwork. It was a good middle-class life, particularly when he was promoted to school principal.

I have seen photos of the young you. What a striking beauty you were, with sharp features and large eyes that made many mistake you for a mixed race or a Eurasian. You had a taste for figure-hugging shift dresses that showed off your curves and shapely legs.

You waltzed into being a housewife. It was a perfectly respectable step, in my view, but it was apparently not one that you had desired for me.

When I was a kid, I could not understand why you did not want me around in the kitchen. That was where you spent most of the day, surrounded by simmering pots, scarred chopping boards and the smells of raw food. Each time I offered to help in the kitchen, you would shoo me away with "Go and study!" Hence, till this day, cooking is as alien to me as playing the bagpipes. But I studied. You taught me to honour learning as a choice, not as a chore; as an opportunity, not as a right.

You may not realise it but I also studied you. From watching you, I learnt many skills that served me for a lifetime: How to be resourceful, how to treat others, how to be resilient.

It has become family legend that you learnt to cook from scratch only after marriage. We were the great beneficiaries of your commitment to the craft. We were not the only ones. You used to cook extra portions for neighbours, sent over personally. It was food diplomacy at its most authentic.

When word of your cooking skills spread in the neighbourhood, some busy career people offered to pay to join us for dinner every day of the week. You charged only a token sum. The regulars were two lawyer bachelor brothers who came with stories from the exciting world outside.

"Family" became a marvellously elastic concept – the number of "brothers" and "sisters" could keep expanding in our home. I think it became literally full house when, by my secondary school years, we had "brothers" from Grace Home, the Christian drug rehabilitation centre, dining with us about once a month.

You pushed the boat out for the "boys" – as we called the reforming drug addicts – who came accompanied by the pastor and two full-time workers. You did not charge, of course. They showed their appreciation by cleaning their plates of every grain of rice, and washing the dishes.

Sitting around the long rectangular table together with them, I often found myself feeling blessed. Blessed, to have this opportunity to be part of this big diverse family, each struggling to be a better person in his own way, and each drawing strength from the other. And blessed to have a mother like you who showed me what it meant to share what little one had, and to treat each and every life, whatever their background, as equally precious.

Then one day, you told me that I would have a roommate. It was Grandma. Grandpa's business had crashed. They lost their fortune. They had to sell their house and move in with us. Thus, I learnt from a young age that material wealth is a precarious thing indeed on which to build one's dreams and self-worth. It can come and go, like the unpredictable weather outside.

From my new roommate, with whom I shared goodnight whispers and kisses, I learnt many other precious lessons. She was so strong, dignified and resilient, even if she must have felt trapped in a life not of her own making. Like you, she, too, wanted for me another life, different from hers, one more independent, more self-directed. She encouraged me to leave for Singapore. It is to my everlasting regret that she did not live to visit Singapore after I started work as a journalist with *The Straits Times* in 1986. She died shortly after.

From you and Grandma, I learnt never to fear hard work and hardship. During our bad patch, you rolled up your sleeves and set up a hawker stall in a coffeeshop. The array of dishes was mouth-watering, from chicken *kunyit* to sambal *kangkong*, and sweet-and-sour fish. It was an education itself, helping you to man the stall during weekends. The stall was a roaring success – many friends turned up to support – but as a business, it failed, because you could not bring yourself to charge them.

Undaunted, you hit on another plan to save the family from financial distress: Set up a catering business from home. That way, money was collected upfront each month. Sounded promising, as orders poured in.

Every lunchtime and dinner, your helpers – Dad, Grandma and myself – would fan out into the neighbourhood to deliver the dishes in stacked three-tier tiffin carriers. I would balance the carriers on my bicycle – four in my front basket and one hanging at each end of the handle bars. Quite a shaky and sloshy ride, I can tell you. I am glad customers did not complain about their soup container arriving sometimes half-empty.

But at the end of each month, when we totted up the numbers, we found ourselves in the red. Dad, the Math expert, traced it to your over-generous portions and choice of expensive dishes. Charity work again. Then you made fragrant *nasi lemak*, wrapped in banana leaves, for our travelling fishmonger to hawk in his mobile van. The best ingredients. Sold out each day. Your profit margin after all that labour? About 5 cents each packet.

Those hard times bound us closer. I so admired your indomitable will and spirit. Okay, you might not have a head for business, but you did not give up easily or wallow in self-pity. Your heart for giving, despite our own hardship, was humbling. It taught me what was more important and lasting in the larger scheme of things.

You cared more about giving your best at whatever you do, rather than about what you would receive in return for your effort. A rare thing in today's dog-eat-dog world.

"Be strong" was your watchword.

You found your calling when you headed the woman's group in church. Its duties, which included visiting the sick in hospitals and the bereaved at home, required you to be strong and stoic. I accompanied you sometimes as a teenager. You would be the one giving strength to the widows, arm around their shoulders. You would be the one helping with the funeral arrangements, with a dry eye for detail. Once, you even helped to bathe the corpse of a close friend. No fuss.

Later, you worked as a full-time worker in a Christian home for disabled children. I painted the wall mural for the hall. It had a rainbow on it.

In Singapore, I found my own rainbow. It was a relief when I got into the National University of Singapore in 1983. For extra pocket money, I gave tuition, and freelanced as a storyteller at a toy department of a shopping centre during weekends. The university gave me a study loan, which I paid back once I started work. What a joy it was to receive my first pay cheque as a journalist. I gave it to you and Dad, in gratitude, but you both returned it to me in a *hongbao*.

It took me several years of frugal living before I saved enough to send both of you for holidays abroad. First a tour to Europe, then Australia.

It took more years – about 10 – before I set aside enough to do my Masters in the London School of Economics. You were so excited when I flew both of you up to London for my graduation in 1998, and then a holiday in the UK. A highlight was riding a punt-boat on the River Cam in Cambridge. I can still hear your lilting laughter rippling through the sunlit air. It was a long way from our hard days in BM.

I would not be where I am, were it not for the moments I watched and learned from you. I discovered these things are important: Compassion, passion, and courage. Compassion for those around us, passion to pursue causes close to our hearts, and courage to take on challenges with gusto.

These lessons stood me in good stead when I joined politics and became a Member of Parliament in 2001. Singapore was then in recession. One of my first projects was to set up a Sunday market in my constituency, Tampines, to help residents, particularly housewives, earn extra income from setting up stalls. It was inspired by your journey.

Thank you for allowing me to steer my own somewhat unconventional journey on my own steam. Despite the prevailing social pressures, you never lectured me to get married and have kids. Once, in my 20s, I had asked you: "How do you know if it is Mr Right?" Your reply: "You just know." I had no clue what you meant until, at 42, I met a wonderful Scotsman, Graham, who brought out the best in me.

He gave up so much for me when he moved from Edinburgh to Singapore after our marriage in 2007. After I retired from politics in 2015, it was my turn. When you waved goodbye to me the last time I left for Scotland, I felt that familiar stab of loss. Then you flashed your gentle smile, just like you did that fateful moonlit night when I first left home in 1980, and it was all right again.

Irene (left) and her mother, Ruth Ng who turns 85 in June 2021

We left behind a lot of things as life moved on. We learnt to travel light. The most precious things we keep sealed in our hearts. This is why, at whatever stage in my life, however changing the seasons, wherever I am in the world, you are always held close.

I am looking outside the window. The rain has stopped. There is a rainbow – no, a double rainbow. I am thinking of you, Mum, and the love between us that no distance can part.

Love always,
Your daughter Irene

Born in Penang, Irene Ng rose to prominence in Singapore, first as an award-winning journalist with *The New Paper* and *The Straits Times*, and then as an independent-minded Member of Parliament. She was a strong advocate for low-wage workers and multiracial equality. She is a Writer-in-Residence at the ISEAS-Yusof Ishak Institute, and the biographer of S. Rajaratnam, a founding leader of modern Singapore. Her book, *The Singapore Lion: A Biography of S. Rajaratnam* (2010), won an Excellence Award for the Best Book/Best Writer at the Asian Publishing Awards. A writer, she is now based in Scotland with her husband, Graham Berry, but Singapore remains the city of her dreams.

When Little Daughters Become Women

Sharda Harrison

Dear Mama,

Mother and Daughter
Our union was written in the stars from the day you summoned me into your mind's eye as a little 12-year-old girl who longed for her daughter to be born. Our union was shaped into skin and held tight by an umbilical cord. Our love bloomed as fresh lotus grew underneath our feet and step by step, we grew together even as we sometimes grew apart, but every step, we learned about each other. We blossomed with the shifting tides and the waxing moon. We explored the spiritual and indulged in rituals. We have lived a long 33 years together, and counting, underneath the same roof. We have howled at the moon spontaneously, laughed and joked and drunk too many glasses of wine together on, oh, so many of our special nights underneath a starry sky. We have cried. We have cried a lot and while we teared, either of us would sit by the side of the other in

order to listen or sometimes just to be and sometimes on a rare occasion, stroke each other's hair. Our union has been a long time coming, of mother and daughter and daughter and teacher, of artist and muse and actress and director or vice versa; we are entwined in the great bosom of the Divine Mother.

What I Love About You

When little girls are little girls, their mothers are their heroes. Then one day, little girls grow up to become little women. That evolution has given us a chance to sit back and either continue to marvel at our mothers, or marvel at how on earth we once treated them as goddesses because as little women, we now see through the rosy veil of "domestic-mumsy" role-play and our eyes zoom straight for the flaws that come with every mother who is really just a struggling human being.

However, to me, you have always been the epitome of a woman. I saw the cracks as I grew up and I appreciated you even more for your raw humanity. I admire and love that you are sensual, courageous, intelligent, and how you speak your mind. You are like a child, dancing in a field of butterflies, or like a monk chanting in a monastery. You are the epitome of fierce femininity and I will forever be here to look up at you in wonder, in amusement, in amazement, in admiration and awe. I believe it is more than fine for a daughter to marvel at her mother, until the day mother and daughter say goodbye, until all this becomes but a memory.

A Memory

Out of all the memories I have of us, I think my favourite is this vision of my brother Sean, you and I at Bukit Timah Nature Reserve which we would visit every other weekend during a period in our childhood. It was your will to teach us how to connect with Nature. I recall us standing at the foot of this gigantic tree on Bukit Timah Hill. Sean and I were little then and we followed your cue. You demonstrated as we watched, with your palms open against the tree trunk, looking up at the canopy above and with a deep inhale and exhale, you closed your eyes, palms out, silently absorbing the energy of the tree. Sean and I followed suit. There we were, the three of us, a mother and her children, with all of our palms pressed against a mighty old tree, staring up at its branches and leaves, smiling sweetly.

I wonder if anyone saw us. I wonder if anyone cared. However, though we were alone in that moment as a family, I also remember feeling like the entire jungle stood with us in that moment. The air was crisp, the sunlight peeking in between your hair, the clouds in the distance, the soft soil underneath my shoes and the crunch of dried leaves. I stood in silence, staring at the sky, but really, I was staring at you, as I continue to do so, even at 33 years of age, how you capture my attention, undivided.

A Divide

If it is not obvious how much I have stated that I love you in this letter, then you might really need to get your eyes checked! Strangely enough, though, I feel more closely connected to you now as a young woman than I had ever been as a child. I felt most of my childhood was stressful, being strewn around emotionally by the great divide between Papa and you. By no means am I putting blame on the divorce for causing Sean and me emotional stress. As children, we understood that this is what life is about! We are human, after all, and we all struggle. Yet, as with any separation, be it Brexit, The Beatles or Marriage, it is the aftermath or consequences that are felt greatly by all those involved.

In this case, it was Sean and I who experienced that very high emotional rollercoaster ride. I felt alone most of the time and I was never sure which parent I was supposed to be raised by. Ultimately, I would come to understand that I would be raised by both of you, but in incredibly different ways. Papa is one of the kindest, most down-to-earth, genuine human beings I know. He would ground me in the logical and scientific aspects of life and you would be my spiritual guide, mentor and sister. Somehow, the great divide acted as a kind of great force which helped all four of us dig deeper into various aspects of our lives and play a "bigger game".

If you think about it, the divorce had propelled you into leaving behind the identity of "wife" and set you on a path of independence, a separation from longing and needing partnership. It forced you to take ownership of your holistic journey back to Nature, plants and medicines. Papa left the Singapore Zoo and played an even more active role as a global conservationist, zoo designer and keynote speaker. Sean and I channelled our inner discomfort into filmmaking and theatre. Both of us have pursued a difficult path in making art, but seem to be doing pretty all right for ourselves! It makes me think with hindsight that perhaps, that divide was the reset towards a new beginning.

A New Chapter Begins

When Grandma passed on, it felt like an entire bus had driven straight through my chest. She was, in many ways, the matriarch of our family and with her passing, our family crumbled and has since not been repaired back to good faith. Grandma Margaret Rodriquez would go on to inspire us to create two plays revolving around her life and death. Perhaps in her passing, we had found some light.

When we travelled to Penang together, I remember that you had an incredible experience when a new name, Ajuntha, was given to you. I felt a great weight lifting off you. I took a step back and again, marvelled. Marvelled at you for being so brave to begin, again. Nazli, the old name, was associated with the pain of your parents, which you had been apparently carrying with you since birth. Thus, with a new name, a new faith and an unclogged channel in your spirit, I truly felt that life did begin again for us in 2015. It was the year we were starting our artistic journey together as mother and daughter. I doubt many mother-daughter duos get to proclaim that they have performed and created art together. Yet with you, it always felt comfortable.

Even when I was beginning my stage career, I had always confided in you about my character work or the philosophical side to my acting journeys. You always seemed to ride the same waves with me and you were, and still are, always here for me, with every new role I receive or show I create. To finally ride that wave professionally together, workshopping our show, *Hayat*, in Bali for a week, practising martial arts every morning, posing for publicity pictures, reading reviews of our work together in the national papers and, of course, actually performing this show, in front of a live audience for a renowned festival, the M1 Fringe Festival 2018 (for which our work was commissioned) was something I will always, always hold dear to me! (So much so that I just had to squeeze all that information into one long sentence!)

In many ways, the year *Hayat* was born was a new beginning for us: All the fighting, screaming at each other, acting and being directed, dealing with tantrums – it was really about inviting each other into a new layer of authenticity.

Being Authentic

This brings me to this word, "authenticity". If it is one thing you and Papa had taught Sean and me, it is to be our true selves. In that respect, both of you, though having raised us separately, were on the same page. You are known to many as the "medicine woman". In the Americas indigenous culture, the term "medicine woman" refers to the shaman of the tribe, a witch or one who knows how to heal her fellow tribesmen through the use of plants. To understand you deeply, is to understand Nature. A plant or an animal cannot be anything more than its primal self. There is little ego involved in the wild nature and order of things. It is through Nature that you encourage us to return to and this has been your life-long mission.

I, again, marvel at your fire and elegance when it comes to dedicating your entire life to the life of plants. You come with no hang-ups or status, without any need for material things like a fancy car or a big house. In that sense, you are very simple in your needs, in order to serve a purpose greater than yourself and you choose to be nothing more and nothing less. That, in itself, is where your power and your greatness lie and through this calling of yours, I have been blessed to be your daughter to realise, at my age, as I struggle through the ups and downs of being a woman in her 30s, to cherish and honour my true self, to be honest and fearlessly authentic.

One of my greatest fears is to not have learnt from you and yet I treat all your knowledge as if it is fossilised forever. The truth is, nothing lasts forever, not even our time together as mother and daughter. Time is short as you approach 70 this year. Death is something we openly discuss and yet, every time I think about "time" and how transient it is, the impermanence of you frightens me.

Death

"Hayat" is a name which means "life" in Arabic. This is ironic, given the entire context of our play – *Hayat* is about a woman in her late 60s coming to terms with the death of her 92-year-old mother, which leads her to prepare for her own inevitable passing. Every time we performed that show and it came to the one moment of breaking the fourth wall, I would turn to look at you and whisper: "I can't imagine living my life without you, Mum."

Even as I type this, I feel my throat swell up because when I think about it, having spent my entire life living with you, our relationship has evolved from mother and daughter into friends and now, sisters. By the natural order of things, I suppose a mother must go before her child and I never hope

Shada Harrison (right) performing with her mother on stage.

for that to be reversed, so as to not have you suffer the pain of losing a child. However, when that day does come, it will be a day of mixed emotions for me.

I am prepared now to learn the ways of the authentic woman and prepare for the chapter we are all moving towards while on Earth – death. I want to be there for your death, to arrange for the prayer and chanting, to assist you in your transition from this world to the next. I want to wash your body after your spirit has left, and kiss your feet and wipe your face and say to you: "I can't imagine living my life without you, Mum." And then whisper yet again: "But I know we will meet again in our ever-evolving eternal life."

I love you.

Always Your Little Daughter,
Sharda

Sharda Harrison is a Singaporean actress and arts educator. Her most recent productions are *The Son* by Pangdemonium Theatre, and *Xalisco, a place,* directed by Ines Somellera for the Cervantino Festival. She runs her own theatre and education company, Pink Gajah Theatre, which she founded in 2013. Her most recent works under Pink Gajah Theatre was *Hayat* for the M1 Fringe Festival 2018 and *VERSO/RECTO* for Centre 42's late-night texting. Sharda is also a theatre lecturer, having attained her Masters in Arts Pedagogy and Practice, and appears regularly on television.

Guilt, Survived

Cheryl Charli Tan

> If a mother was Sacrifice personified, then a daughter was Guilt, with no possibility of redress.
>
> Milan Kundera
> *The Unbearable Lightness of Being*

You wonder why I always start all my Mother's Day cards with an apology; why every card I give to you on your birthday or mine, reads "Thank you for giving birth to me", "I am sorry I have disappointed you" and "I hope I make you proud one day". You wonder why I even give you cards on my birthday; why, when they ask, I tell my friends that it is you, and not me, who should be celebrated; why I simply want to disappear every January. For what is there to seek repentance? Why is my existence something I feel compelled to atone for? What has this to do with you?

Everything.

The required price to pay to raise a child is absolute. This is the one fixed price. There are no negotiations. You were required to surrender everything – past, present, and future. If all you could give at present constituted everything you had, then surrendering your future, too, would mean that the requirement to raise a child was everything and more. How do you decide to surrender what you do not know? What if having me in the future cost you more than you were prepared to give? What if it left you with nothing?

It is not a very good investment, is it? How do you bank so much – an unknowable amount – on something that does not guarantee a solid ROI? As I navigate early adulthood, I am starting to realise that we do not live by logic alone, but by unspeakable grace undeserved. There are things in this world that cannot be explained or rationalised away by the brightest of minds or the logic that lines our world's most widely observed and obeyed systems. An investment is a limited, controlled risk taken with a clear, certain promise. A daughter is an unlimited, uncontrolled risk taken, with an uncertain promise and a potential for pain and disappointment that could well extend over the rest of your life. A child is the life investment that promises no returns, yet demands all you possibly have to offer, complete with every hidden cost, terms and conditions be damned. A child is the art project that will occupy your heart and mind, day and night, for the rest of your life. It is the project you cannot bail out of. "Mother" is the title you cannot strip away, the character you cannot step out of offstage when the show is over. Why have a child? Why have me?

***

You are a wall.
A wall I lean on. A wall that shelters me.
A wall to which I have, for years, whispered all the secrets of my breaking heart.
A wall that listens.
A wall that keeps me out.

You, with your trinkets of remembrance and your fading photographs. You, with your past, your secrets and pain, suppressed anxieties and fears. You, silent at the dining table, eyes glistening hopefully as we scoop the food you have spent the entirety of two days to prepare. You, apologising (to my horror) yet again, because it was a tad too salty to someone's liking. You, every night on your bed, iPad propped up before you, filling the silence with another show you have discovered. You never let me in. You never let me see how much you hurt, alone. You, a wall, protecting me. From the world. From myself.

You are a wall I hit, with raised voices and careless words you never deserve, with all of my outlandish dreams and preposterous passions that lead nowhere. Years and years of 2am fights with me crying over the dining table, will never make you understand why I consciously choose a path that makes my life harder than it needs to be. Still, I wake up the morning after, puffy-eyed, and still head to the theatre for rehearsals. I come home late, to your dismay. For years now, I have begun to build my home in the corners of empty blackbox spaces instead of in your arms. I no longer plead for you to carry me on your shoulders while I fight my monsters. Mine is the passion you will never understand. And yours is the face I will still search for in every crowd, in every audience, when the curtain calls.

***

You used to know me.

You knew me, at every stage of my life. You knew the struggle I had with schools, the fights I got into with boys on the bus in kindergarten, how I used to steal Powerpuff Girls stationery because I wanted things badly. You knew all the people I had ever wished to be – the astronaut, the archaeologist, the figure skater, the chemist, the historian, the linguist, the lawyer, the theatre artist. You used to know me. As the years pass, you know me still, albeit an uglier version of me as I begin to learn that this world is cruel. You know me crying on the floor at night screaming, thinking aloud how it would be better to die than to keep breaking your heart this way. You save me from myself. Who saves you from yours?

These days, I try not to think about you too much. I end up crying otherwise. Your abundance of love, forgiveness, and grace, is a testimonial to how much I will always lack. I spill my tears and secrets into the hands of strange lovers who promise me the world, then break my heart in the same breath. Then I come running home with the ashes of my burnt bridges and broken heart, and place them on your altar of grace.

There are times I think of the weight that is not mine to carry. The weight that you have spent 23 years carrying on your own. I think of your heart – it is shattering, it is resilient. I think of death, and your brushes with it, your witnessing, your grief. Your love demands sacrifice – yours.

In order to love me, you had to sacrifice everything. This story is nothing new – every mother is demanded sacrifice. It is a prerequisite in raising a child. But yours demanded more. It demanded smiling reassuringly at me for years as the earth trembled and the building collapsed around you, as you fought to move on and find yourself in the arms of another man who would shelter us for the years to come, as you find yourself in silences sometimes too deafening to drown out, how we have taken you for granted, lying in a cesspool of neglect. Why did having me mean losing the one you loved most at that time, the one you were supposed to spend the rest of your life with? Why did having me, from the get-go, require that kind of sacrifice?

Whose blood ritual are we unwilling participants of?

***

There is much of the world I have not tasted. There are tears yet to spill, my heart yet to break, grace yet to know. There is much of life I will never know, but I do know this: I know what it means to love, because you have loved me. Perhaps in another life, we would never have known each other. I would never call you my mother. Perhaps it is redundant when I tell you I would find you and choose you as my mother in every life I will ever live, if we do live to see another life. Perhaps it is redundant thinking; I understand love and sacrifice because I have seen how much you have given to love me, because what I understand is only being on the receiving end of your ultimate sacrifice. Perhaps all I will ever feel is guilt, for being your daughter, for being born. And perhaps there will never be a way to "pay you back", because your love is as boundless

Cheryl (right) skiing with her mother.

as the sea. I am beginning to understand that sometimes, life gives us things we must bear the consequences of having. Dear Mummy, you are Love, personified.

I must learn to be content with being loved in this life infinitely more than I deserve.

Cheryl Charli Tan is a multi-disciplinary theatre artist. Some recent works include illustrating the poetry collection, *Oddballs, Screwballs and Other Eccentrics* (2020), in collaboration with poet Felix Cheong. Theatre credits include *Anything Can Happen, Something Must Happen* (2019) with W!LDRICE, directed by Edith Podesta, *The Moon Is Less Bright* (2018) by The Second Breakfast Company, and *Without Reason* (2017) directed by Adib Kosnan, commissioned by M1 Peer Pleasure. She is also passionate about how technology and programming, AI and machine learning, can be integrated into making or generating art and experiences.

I Am My Mother's Son

William Phuan

Dear Ma,

Your heart stopped beating at 10.01pm on February 9, 2015. I had just stepped into the hospital room, and the whole family was already there. Sis turned to me and said you were gone. It then became a blur of activity, with nurses and doctors going in and out of the room, asking questions and unplugging medical equipment.

Mercifully, I had a quiet moment with you before they pushed you to the mortuary. Our helper, Sudarsi, was with me in the room. She had been caring for you for the past six years. This tiny and stoic woman, who somehow managed to find the strength to lift you from the bed to the wheelchair, every day, all by herself.

She started combing your hair, the last time she knew she would be able to do that. I took a warm towel and wiped your face, eyes, mouth, ears. We knew you would want to be primped up, the inconvenience of death notwithstanding.

I dabbed lavender oil on your face, gently massaging your skin so that your skin would still be moisturised in the cold chamber and you would still smell good.

But your mouth just would not close. Try as we could, your lips kept stubbornly apart, leaving your mouth agape as if you were gasping for air. We took out your dentures, thinking that they were getting in the way. But no matter what we did, it just would not work. The muscles holding your jaw, like the rest of your body, had all gone to sleep forever.

The night before, I had kept vigil in your room. You had already slipped into your morphine-induced state of unconsciousness, slowly, peacefully drifting away. I had fitful moments of sleep, as I constantly got up to check that you were still breathing – still alive, still with us.

For as long as I could remember, I was always haunted by the spectre of your death. You had had many near-death moments ever since your aneurysm 20 years ago, but you always pulled through by your sheer willpower. When I was eight, you were rushed to A&E for a sudden bout of appendicits. I remember that you were in so much pain that I thought you were going to die. For a few days, Sis and I were left at home with Grandpa, while you and Pa were in the hospital. I thought I would never see you again. When we finally visited you, the expression on your face – a mix of relief, pain, fear, worry – was forever seared in my mind as you lay lifeless on the hospital bed. The fear of hospital, illness, and losing you was locked forever in my psyche since.

Another moment triggered that fear again when I was 12. You received a frantic call from our aunt in Kuala Lumpur, who broke the news that your youngest sister had just died in a freak electrocution accident at home. You went into the room and bawled, and did not come out for a long time. I thought you had fainted inside. You quickly packed your bags, made a few arrangements for us, and took the train to KL the next day to tend to your sister's family. I was gripped with fear that something could happen to you during the trip, or that you could be electrocuted too. While nothing untoward happened in the end, in my young childish mind though, you never seemed to be that far from the snares of death.

As I watched over you in the hospital room while you drew in deep, soothing breaths, I realised that I had never told you how proud I was to be your son. I am my mother's son, through and through. My calm and gentle demeanour – that is you. My quiet strength and determination – that is you too. My love of fashion and my vanity – that is totally you.

I grew up playing with dolls but I never had a Barbie (I never had a thing for them, for some reason). I inherited some of Sis' dolls, but I would also ask you to buy me new ones. My favourite was the Batgirl doll, with her luscious red hair, voluptuous body, skin-tight Lycra costume and yellow boots. Then I started adding figurines of *Star Wars* characters to my collection: The likes of Boba Fett, Princess Leia, C-3PO, and Bib Fortuna. All these dolls and figurines became part of the menagerie of characters for my own pretend world.

I loved you for never batting an eyelid whenever I asked you to buy me a new doll, sew costumes for them (based on my own design), or let me use your dress jewellery for the costumes. There was no questioning or doubtful look on your face, in spite of some grumblings from Pa and Grandpa. But you would always go along with my requests, however outrageous they might be, in your quiet, good-humoured way.

I would pick up some leftover fabrics from your own dressmaking, and ask you to turn them into some period dresses for my characters. My favourite clothing was inspired by the Tang and Ming dynasties, while my dolls would be steeped in martial arts and period drama, gliding in the world of *jianghu*. I would use your gold and silver chains, brooches and rings to create elaborate headdresses for the characters, sometimes so heavily ornamented that they could have snapped off the dolls' necks if they were not made of plastic.

You were so talented in your sewing skills that sometimes I thought you could have started your own business as a seamstress. No matter, I found a perfect collaborator in you who nurtured my love for clothing, design and all things beautiful.

When I was in the army, I got into the phase for chiffon (do not ask me why). For my ORD (Operationally Ready Date) dinner and dance event – to leave the army with a bang – I designed this black top with a bare-back cut-out, in the shape of an inverted V and covered with chiffon. We went to the second floor of the People's Park Food Centre (a misnomer for a place that sells sundries, fabrics and all) to find the right chiffon and materials. Then you promptly got down to work to wield your magic in creating the top. Needless to say, it was fabulous and it remains one of the most cherished pieces of clothing that you had created for me (right up there with the emerald green satin-silk pants).

After you were gone, I was reminded of the gift of your sewing skills again. Sister Geraldine from the Nativity Church Centre in Hougang told me that you often volunteered to help sew the religious uniforms for the sisters, as well as the cushion covers at the centre. They were so grateful for your generous gesture, but even more impressed by your skills. And this was despite you being wheelchair-bound for the past 20 years. Yet, you remained determined to keep up your craft and use the sewing machine as your tool of charity, wheelchair be damned.

The next health scare came in 1994 and it altered all our lives for good. It was May 8, Mother's Day. I remember being woken up by Pa, who found you lying semi-conscious on the floor. You were already all dressed up to go to church, but you were moaning and groaning that you had a terrible headache. I held your hand and it was stone cold. We called the ambulance, which immediately took you to Tan Tock Seng Hospital. My worst fear of you dying came rushing up again.

They found that you had a brain aneurysm and had to quickly operate on you. The operation went on forever. You were not out of the operation room until the next day. Waiting in the endlessly long hospital corridor, breathing in the arid antiseptic air made me feel even more desperate and forlorn.

We finally saw you in the ICU after your operation. It looked like a surreal scene from a sci-fi movie. There were all kind of tubes running through your body and wires attached to different machines, each monitoring a function of your organs. It was as if they had pieced you back together, limb by limb, after an accident, a la Robocop. I had often pondered if you were conscious of your state then: Was your soul hovering above your body, and wondering if you should go back in, or leave forever?

But you were not out of the woods yet. The doctors told us that you had a massive rupture, which left you paralysed from the waist down and severely damaged the nerves of your hands. You would be an invalid for the rest of your life. We prayed fervently for your recovery, but we were also worn out by the endless waiting and the bleak situation.

Yet you amazed and surprised us with your strength and life force. You showed us that you were a fighter. The meek and gentle disposition belied a woman of remarkable determination and stoicism. You woke up, and you came back into our world. I held your hand and thanked you for coming back.

It was a long and hard six months of recovery, filled with tears, setbacks and frustrations. But you endured all of it and pulled yourself up, time and again, even when you were on the verge of giving up endless times. I could not understand fully the pain and anguish that you were going through then, until I read your diary recently. You suffered from enormous physical toll, but what tortured you most was feeling useless and that you were a burden to all of us. But you also wrote about the grace of God, who kept you alive and made you feel alive. You wrote about being grateful.

You pushed yourself through physiotherapy to learn how to sit up, how to turn your body, how to hold a spoon – all the basic actions that you had to relearn as if you were a child. You wanted to get well desperately because you wanted to take care of us again. You showed me the length a mother would go for the love of her children and family. It hurt me to see you so helpless at times, but I also knew, deep down, that you were a survivor. My survival skills – they are all yours too.

For the next 20 years, you learnt how to navigate the world and live your life wheelchair-bound. Initially, you did not want to go out as you were conscious of how people were looking at you. You refused to go to church, the market, the hawker centre, the shopping malls. Not anywhere. Nowhere. You just wanted to stay at home. It took some urging, baiting, admonishing and even bribing. Then you realised that you still had a life ahead of you – your children and grandchildren wanted you to be fully in their lives – that you finally took a roll outside.

I have never told you this, but when I was living in New York, I looked forward to your phone call every day. You would call me every night, around 10pm or 11pm, and we would chat about our day. You would tell me about what was going on at home, what the grandkids were up to, what the weather was like in Singapore. All the mundane things, yet they were balm to my homesick heart. Your calls were like the lullaby before my sleep, luring me with sweet thoughts of home and family. Sometimes, when I was sick, especially during the flu season in winter, I would call you to get some long-distance pampering – the good old nagging from you telling me to take my medication and drink lots of soup.

I loved sending you and the family all kinds of cards: Christmas, birthday, Chinese New Year. And I loved receiving them too. Your unsteady handwriting brought me so much joy that it made up for the distance that kept us apart. My years in New York were one of the best times of my life, but

I also knew that those were the times that you missed me the most. How I wished fervently then I could bring you to New York to experience it so that you could understand why I wanted to make something of my life there. I like New York in June, how about you?

Three years after your death, I shared with a friend about how I was relieved that you were gone. She has an acute sense of the spiritual realm, and she told me she saw that my heart was covered by a light, white veil. She said it was like a cloak of sadness that seemed to weigh my heart down. I immediately teared up. How could she have seen it? When you died, I was genuinely happy and comforted that you were finally freed from your suffering. But I was also overcome with regret and guilt at not being a good son to you during your last years. I had been carrying this guilt with me all this while. But you had never held it against me. My friend said you were ready to help me lift the veil off, but I had to forgive myself and let it go. You wanted my heart to beat as strongly and fully as it ever could.

Your death is the gift that keeps giving. During my own grieving and healing, I realised that I was following your own journey of grieving and healing from your condition. God's gentle and loving hand had guided us both from the valleys of hurt and loss, and led us into His embrace of love and hope. He showed me how unconditional your love is, which allows me the forgiveness and peace that I never thought that I could ever deserve.

Your death also gives me the gift to offer solace and support to friends who are experiencing the pain of losing loved ones themselves. You give me the words of comfort, something that I have felt deeply myself, that I could share with them. You teach me how to lend a listening ear to them, how to be present and just provide relief by my presence.

I love you so much, Ma, and I miss you so much. Yet I know there is not a day that passes without you still looking out for me from heaven. I remember the four days of wake that were held after your death. Every night was filled with people – your friends from church, neighbours, all our cousins and friends. Every night was a celebration of your life and the mark you made on all our lives. I do not know if you had felt it then, but it was a joyful time. Everyone remarked how serene and contented you looked, dressed in the white blouse that you had previously picked out yourself. I do think that you were basking in all the affection and joy during those nights. It made me so grateful and happy to be your son. God has blessed me with you as my mother.

I am my mother's son. I am proud to be your son.

William Phuan is the Executive Director of the Singapore Book Council, a non-profit dedicated to developing and promoting Singapore's books and writers. He was formerly the director of The Arts House, and Programme Director of the New York Asian American International Film Festival. William has extensive experience working in various sectors, including journalism, arts policy and film curation in both the US and Singapore. William has also lectured part-time on arts management and film.

A photo with my Ma at the Botanic Gardens when I was 14.

An outing to Kusu Island with my Ma and sister when I was six.

Celebrating the combined birthdays of my Pa, Ma and niece in September 2000. (They are all Virgos.)

A Magic Pearl

Lydia Kwa

October 31, 2020

Dear Mum,

This morning, soon after I woke up, I sneezed three times in quick succession, just like you used to. You have not disappeared, have you?

It is a crisp autumn day in my neighbourhood in east Vancouver. Before dawn, seagulls and crows own the park below, their cliques and chat groups a private language inaccessible to humans. Much later, Mr Gongfu appears around 8.30am, to run through his various drills, a combination of grace, strength and skill.

Watching him, I could not help but think that you could not move with such ease and confidence through your life. You usually held your body in, tightly, as if you were bound by invisible ropes. You often spoke in a low, grumbling tone, if you were cross or angry, but hesitatingly. You were a female of your generation, unable to move with the kind of confidence my neighbour Mr Gongfu possesses. Despite such constraints, your manner was often brusque, free of sentiment or pretensions.

You showed flashes of mischief, despite your usual sombre presentation. I would like to think I got some of my cheekiness from you. I remember you saying, one of the times I went to visit you and stayed for five weeks, before I returned to Vancouver: "*Di see gao, tapi di siang bey.*" *You may be born in the Year of the Dog, but you are like a Horse.* You noticed how much I liked to go out and check out new things; whereas you, also a Dog, 24 years older, liked to stay close to home.

Love, I learned from you, is not a sentiment; it does not consist of flattery. Love is a firm investigation of how your bowels are doing. An offer of Kleenex or a clean towel. A bowl of bitter Chinese medicinal brew, sometimes with a pig brain sitting in the centre of the dark brown liquid.

What could I offer you in return? Not much, in comparison. I visited you when I could, I sent you money, I called you once a week. I found a helper to assist you, in the last four months of your life. I even overrode your protests not to hire someone: "*Mai lah, siuh gui.*" *No, it is too expensive.*

I am grateful I was there, keeping you company in the last week of your life.

Life has changed drastically without you. Every cell in me requires realignment. I have stepped into a void that demands my curiosity.

Has it been three years since you left? I understand that you did not feel you could read those books I had written. But you were my first listener when I was a child.

You had been the one I went to, after school, to recount the day's experiences – whom I met, what happened, who was evil toward me, who was nice. You listened, as you plucked the roots off *tau gay* or as you sipped your cup of *kopi-o*. You rarely said anything back. But you would occasionally pause in your plucking of bean sprouts, to nod or moan in empathy. You understood that to listen, one has to attend, if nothing else. I learned that silence could mean so many things.

Since I have your attention – how about I make up a story for you now?

***

A young man of 21, the son of a wealthy Hakka businessman in Singapore, was summoned by his father one day. He was told that arrangements were being made to find him a suitable wife. He bowed to his father, expecting this news. He would fulfill his duties. His betrothed soon arrived from Riau, Indonesia, and a grand wedding ensued, conducted in the traditional Chinese style.

The young man and his wife got along well enough. It is impossible to say what was in their minds when they discovered that she was pregnant. They named their daughter Khim after she was born. Khim was the Hakka word for "piano". I suppose they might have had aspirations for her to be musically inclined. They took delight in their newborn. The young man's father, however, did not like the fact that his son lavished such attention on a mere girl. The patriarch arranged for the baby to be sent away to the mother's mother in Indonesia.

The infant suffered the pain of separation from her parents. Later, when she was almost three, she was brought back into the home, shortly after her brother was born. But the damage had been done. Her spirit was dampened by the poison of rejection. She grew up feeling unloved, concluding that it was her mother who had rejected her.

Although she was an obedient child, a fierce vitality burned inside Khim, but found no outlet. Years later, as an eight-year-old, while at the beach in Katong, Khim found a magic pearl in the midst of the driftwood and seaweed washed up on the shore. She knew it was magical because of the way it gleamed, even on such an overcast day. The pearl called to her: "Khim, Khim." How could the pearl know her name? She quickly placed it inside her dress pocket. Her mother and brother, along with the amah, were paying attention to the flock of swallows overhead.

Khim began, from that day on, to retreat into her private world, in which she could make up stories that comforted her. She could tell the magic pearl these stories, and hence feel less alone.

Months later, the Japanese invaded Singapore. Most inhabitants of the country suffered deprivation and hardship. Khim was afraid of the Japanese troops, even the officers who visited their home on Chapel Road. She noticed how deferential her father and grandfather were to the officers, who came often to their home to dine. There would be delivery of sacks of rice, dried fish and vegetables; sometimes there would be fresh pomfrets and live prawns. Khim saw the differences between how they lived and how others were suffering.

After the Japanese lost the war and left the island, her father seemed very cross. He took out all the Japanese paper currency from the sandalwood trunk, and had the notes burned in a large urn, in the front garden.

Khim was smart, did well in school but she was prevented from going beyond Secondary two — her mother said Khim should focus on learning how to be good at household chores and cooking, in preparation for her eventual role as a wife. Khim seethed with resentment. She performed her household chores grudgingly. She became obsessed with being perfect in performing her chores; but try as hard as she did, she never gained praise from her mother.

Khim continued to talk to the magic pearl about the injustices she suffered. She was bored with having to do the right things. After all, it seemed there was nothing she could do to make Ah Mak happy.

Khim grew up to be very beautiful. Men started to pay attention to her. Her mother wanted to match her with a wealthy Hakka man. But Khim thought he was extremely ugly and boring. One date was enough.

She chose to marry a handsome Hokkien man who serenaded her with romantic songs at Katong Park. Songs that he had learned from watching Mario Lanza movies. She herself had a squeaky, singing voice; she felt drawn to the beautiful baritone voice of her suitor. He also played the piano well; perhaps it was fated, she reasoned, by having been named Khim. She agreed to marry Huan when he proposed.

Life soon lost its romantic tinge when she experienced Huan's tendency to demand her utmost attention. He sulked if she refused to have sex with him. He cajoled her, and she often gave in. Huan shouted at her. He experienced her lack of interest as a rejection. The foetus inside Khim felt the waves of his violence pass through the uterine wall to her.

Huan liked playing with his child. Khim had fleeting glimpses of her own father revelling in her presence. The memory was intolerably painful. Khim sometimes felt herself detached from the little one. She did not understand why she vacillated between feelings of tenderness and numbness.

Khim continued to seek out her magic pearl and talk to it.

Out in public life, Huan was charming and attentive. At home, he was an entirely different person, often morose and easily angered. He would sometimes strike out at Khim and his daughter, feeling the victim of rejection.

There were many dark moments in married life for Khim. Sometimes, she wished she could end her life; she confided her despair to the pearl. But she could not bring herself to do it, because there was this young daughter needing her care. She was flooded with memories of her own mother loving her brother much more than her. She tried to hush the inner voices that said that if not for the child, she would have left Huan and become a free woman.

One night, the pearl came to her in a dream. This time, instead of hovering above her, it came to rest gently next to Khim's head on the pillow. "If you swallow me, I will make you strong and powerful and able to leave this world of suffering."

Khim woke up with a shudder. Huan was on his side, back turned, snoring loudly. She got up and went into the kitchen. She poured herself a cup of hot water from the thermos. Sat down and sipped and wondered: What if it is true?

The next day, when her husband was at work and the child was at school, she took the pearl out and decided to take the risk. There was nothing to lose. She swallowed the tiny pearl with some kopi-o, instantly felt light-headed and went to bed to lie down.

When she woke up, she was a young girl again, alone at the beach, looking out at the ocean, the pearl shimmering in the palm of her right hand. She might have looked like the eight-year-old she had been, but she remembered everything she had experienced throughout her life until that moment.

It was low tide. She made up her mind. She would walk away from the shoreline, and the walking would take her somewhere else in place and time. She would never have to live according to what ensued later in her adulthood. Somewhere out there, in the far horizon, there was another life waiting for her.

***

January 1, 2021

Dear Mum,

I have been thinking, if you had been still alive through the Covid-19 pandemic, it would have been terrible for you to be there in Singapore and I, here in Canada, separated from you. Or – even if you had lived another 10 months beyond October 2017 – it would have been very painful for you to know that I was diagnosed with breast cancer, and underwent surgery and chemotherapy in 2018 and 2019.

This morning, when I woke up, I sensed your presence at the edges of my breathing, your face drawn close to mine. You were sniffing at me, like a mother dog would do with her puppy.

I recall that photo of the two of us, in those gigantic, floppy hats. Where and when was that? We were either in Malacca or Penang, on holiday. A moment of joy!

Today marks the beginning of a new year on the Gregorian calendar. Does a new year signal a sudden, magical turn? Or perhaps, there are other possible forms of magic. What do you think? You might say: *"Di siao si bo?" Are you crazy?*

It is a misty winter morning as I continue this letter to you. I would like to think your *hun* soul lingers, protecting me. There is not a day I do not think of you.

I have lived more than six decades. I can finally voice the vague, sensed shadows and things left unsaid in your lifetime. You were starved for love. Unfulfilled promises and numerous betrayals hurt your sensitive nature so much that you walled yourself in, to stay protected. I feel a similar stiffening reluctance often materialise in me, that familiar wariness. And yet, I resolve to live beyond that narrative. I wish to take you with me on new adventures.

I recall a time when you were 60 – our trip to Chinatown, your delight as you posed with the pomelo clasped in both hands, in front of your belly. Your beaming smile and the gleam in your eyes. Your spirit had been undoubtedly dimmed by the trauma you had experienced from infancy on – yet, you remained capable of simple pleasures. You cuddled that pomelo as if it were your baby, with a confident, easy embrace.

Are such moments ever simple? Did you have a magic pearl tucked away in your being?

Where is the end, I wonder? From the time I began to form in your womb, to the point at which you left your

Lydia (right) and her mother, having fun on holiday in Malaysia, 1970s.

physical form as my mother, I grew to become the mother who conceives of you as beyond those restrictions of form. Here, looking out at the mist as it lifts from my world of experience, I feel a gentle awakening. I take you with me into my own dying, as we travel along paths you could not have travelled before.

You are gone but you have not disappeared.

Lydia Kwa was born in Singapore and lived there until she left for Canada to study psychology in 1980. She has published two books of poetry and four novels. Her fourth novel, *Oracle Bone*, was published by Arsenal Pulp Press in 2017 as the first novel in the *chuanqi* 傳奇 trilogy. A new version of the second book, *The Walking Boy* (Arsenal Pulp Press), was released in spring 2019. She is currently working on the third novel in this trilogy.

Dear Jenny

Regina De Rozario

Dear Jenny,

They have asked me to write you a letter. Some short story I could share about the relationship we have had, or perhaps the way we parted and how the time we have spent apart feels. I must admit that this has been something that I had to sit with for a while, and even this first paragraph is taking me far too long to write. Too many starts and stops between the first line and this point. It does not matter how I try to approach this task: Whether I try to write by hand or type in long streaming sentences, every word feels inadequate, destined to be deleted, crumpled, or erased.

How do you say hello to someone you have been longing to see? How do you say goodbye again?

I am writing to you at a strange time. We are in the middle of a pandemic. The climate is off-kilter. The world as you left it has changed so much. We alternate between praying for the best and preparing for the worst; between keeping an eye on the dramatic headlines of the daily news and just getting on with the mundane urgencies of every day.

The people you left behind have changed too. Keith and Gwen and their families are doing fine, so you need not worry. The children are all grown up now, and I see pieces of you in them and their own children. Pieces of the woman I knew when I was a child. Pieces of your smile and your laugh.

In myself, I see other pieces of you in the mirror in the morning; in my haze of sleepiness, in the moments before I have my coffee. I hear your older voice in my voice when I say "Good morning". An uttered acknowledgment, shaking myself awake, bracing myself for another day. Not smiling. No laugh.

The pandemic has made it necessary for us to stay at home for weeks on end. The hours meld, and the days feel endless. Every morning, I find myself checking the calendar to remember what day of the week it is. Lately, every day feels like a Monday after a long weekend. Tired, and dragged out. My days are filled with busyness but ironically, I begin each one feeling like I did not get enough done the day before and not quite knowing what I should prioritise in the next.

If you choose not to, it is possible not to see or speak to anyone at all. These days, I keep to myself and try to get my work done. I avoid crowds and unnecessary conversations. I am a rock, as you used to sing to me, I am an island.

You can imagine then, how easy it is in this isolation, to spend much of my time these days in my head, letting the fragments of the present day fall into place alongside fragments of the days that have passed. They all seem to fit effortlessly, and they all seem to lead me back to you.

The wind is belting the windows. It has not stopped raining since Sunday.

I cannot remember the last time I walked in the rain, or breathed in the wind, unmasked and unencumbered, feeling it tingle the hairs on my neck, or cool against my bare face. I do remember the walks we used to take from our house to the seaside, well before the seaside was pushed aside by the highway and our house was shuttered and demolished and our address expunged from the street directory. I remember the seaside, the way its scent would hit us even before we arrived. Waters sparkling under the sun, green like glass. That kite you made out of tracing paper, cellophane and bamboo, that I never learned how to fly. Keith and Gwen were so much better at it. I would drag my paper diamond across the grass but never quite fast enough for the wind to whip it into the sky.

Keith and Gwen were so much better at things. Running, cycling, all manner of sports and games. "Well, they are older than you," you would say to me, which was an assurance when I was five, but became less so by the time I got to 10. For years, I was always the last to come in any race. Rarely picked for any team. Still hopeless at kite-flying. "All my children are different and special in their own way," you said, that one day when I came home from school, upset that I had lost at either "zero point" or hopscotch or some other de rigueur recess sport. It was the kind of thing every mother would say to her child but it was the way that you said it as you held my head close to your chest. Your words, punctuated by your heartbeat, followed by your slow drag on your cigarette. I paced my breathing with yours, every exhalation building belief.

These days, I strain to remember what it is like to be outside, bare-faced, breathing in the wind. But then I think about that silly kite and my attempts at flying it, and your words of belief in me, no matter my failure at something so simple, I cannot help but smile.

***

Jenny – I have only ever called you by your name once. That morning in the hospital when I arrived at your room and found you sitting up in bed, but with your body slumped slightly forward, head limp, eyes closed.

"Good morning," I uttered, at a volume loud enough to wake any sleeping person. "She is up," I said to the nurse who stood at the other side of the room, folding your blanket. I must have surprised or confused her because she stared blankly at me for a second, and then dropped the blanket and left the room without a word.

"Mum, I am here. I am back," I said, sitting on the bed next to you, taking your hand. You did not fold your fingers around mine and your eyes remained closed. I knew then, but disbelief compelled me to say your name. Not louder, for I knew I could no longer wake you, but a whisper: "Jenny." And then I let your hand go.

We always knew – Keith, Gwen and I, that it would be cancer that would take you. You were always good at taking care of us, but we never understood why you could not do the same for yourself. I recognised over time that the cigarettes were a part of that front that you had built for yourself. Jenny, only daughter, mission schoolgirl, working mother, raising three children at a time where women like you were asked to stop at two. You did almost everything they asked you to. You needed something for yourself.

I remember one particular day. This was shortly before we had to move away from our old house. It was in the middle of the day, in the midst of packing up the things in our kitchen, you had an argument with your husband. Something about the things you wanted to keep and the things he wanted to throw away. I was too young to understand the words but I was familiar with the volume and tone – clanging and cruel, punctuated with pauses that chilled the room. You stopped it short by taking me by the hand and briskly walking out of the door. And then lifting me in your arms, carrying me, while you kept walking without stopping until you reached the beach.

You lifted me up onto the breakwater first and told me to sit down. You then clambered up, drew your lighter and pack of cigarettes from your pocket, stared for a while at the horizon before sitting down next to me. I remember watching you, wondering what would happen next, since we were clearly not here to fly kites. I remember the wind was belting our faces, green water foaming at the bottom of the breakwater, sending wafts of salt air upwards. You smoked one cigarette after another as you stared steadfastly ahead. I remember understanding I needed to stay with you, to keep quiet, to not ask questions, even as the time passed as I started to feel hungry. I watched groups of other children running up and down the sand. I counted the ships that floated slowly across the waters.

As the shadows got longer, you finally spoke. "You know, we may never come back here again," you said, exhaling, still staring ahead. "And even if we do," you continued, as you extinguished your cigarette, "this place will never be the same. They are pushing the sea out. We will forget we are an island."

It was nearly dark by the time we got back. Father was moving more things out of the house. A pile of things, we surmised, that we would not be taking with us. You looked at the pile and said nothing, moving past him and exchanged no further words for the rest of the evening. I looked at the pile and noticed my kite balanced at the top of it, freshly broken and askew.

We moved out a week later, to set up our new home, in a new flat, in a new town. You were right, we never went back to the seaside, you and me.

Not every memory of you speaks of loss. I think about the times you would stay up nights with me as I studied until 3 in the morning. You would read the newspaper, work through the crossword, or play solitaire. We did not speak to each other, but I found you a comfort. Even on nights when I did not have to study for exams, I stayed up anyway, and we would sit and read together, or listen to the BBC World Service in the background.

I think about the times we danced together in the living room to The Beatles and The Beach Boys. You singing along to Simon & Garfunkel. Your attempts to teach me the twist or some other dance from your heyday. Your smile as you pinned up the pictures I painted for you, and the silly one-person plays I would write and act out and force you to sit through. Your sigh when I first told you that I was in love with a girl. "Well," you uttered in acknowledgment, pulling my head close to your chest. "I always knew you were going to be different."

***

I should never have left the hospital that night. You had been in for more than a week, not quite recovering. We were told to pray for the best, but to prepare for the worst. Keith, Gwen and I took turns. I would take the evening visiting hours and stay overnight. Sometimes reading next to you, sometimes humming, sometimes calming you with a prayer when you said you were afraid, sometimes lying with you in your bed, holding your head against my chest, patting your back, watching it rise and fall as you fell asleep. But that particular night, you said you wanted to sleep early, that it was better for me to sleep in my own bed. And so I left.

A collage of Regina's growing up years with her mother.

The truth is, Jenny, I have been letting the hours meld for a while now. Well before this pandemic and this need to isolate for safety reasons. I fill the hours with busywork. I have found it a good way of putting some time and distance in-between myself and the day I lost you. To push the sea out, but not wanting to forget. People have asked to see me, and we make plans to get together, but I have always managed to devise an explanation to stay away, to not have to respond to the inevitable "How are you?" One day, I will be ready but as they say, for now, this distance is necessary for safety. And a rock feels no pain, and an island never cries.

This rain is slowing down to a drizzle. It is nearly 2am but from where I sit I can see windows that are still lit. I wonder if anyone is up, listening to music, or learning how to dance, or playing solitaire.

I miss you in these hours, Jenny, as they meld and lead me to another day.

Love,
Gina

Regina De Rozario is an artist and writer from Singapore. Her practice and research interests include psychogeography and how the city shapes the narrative spaces we inhabit. She is also active as one-half of Perception3, an interdisciplinary art duo that explores the notions of loss and memory through text, photography, digital video and site-specific installation.

Thank You, Mummy*

Rose Marie Sivam

Dear Mummy,

I hope I am able to tell you all that I have wanted to. There are so many things to thank you for that a letter will not cover all of them and yet, I wonder why I have not said thank you enough all these years.

But now, seeing you frail, yet calm as if with a secret knowing, I feel I must say some things, even if you knew them already. I did not imagine seeing you in the same hospital where you had started your nursing career, this time as a patient. It is beautiful to see the nurses you had once taught and groomed, now in senior positions, rushing from their different wards to see you, from the moment they heard you were admitted.

I remember accompanying you along these same hospital corridors when I was just five. Now they are spruced up and

---

*Adapted from a letter read to my mother at the Singapore General Hospital five days before she passed on in 2007. She smiled a lot as I read it to her, in-between tears and laughter, with my sister by her side.

the hospital has extended wings and new buildings. In those days, I would try to hold your hand and stake a claim on you while you went about your ward rounds. You would gently tell me: "I am on duty. We cannot hold hands." Still, you let me hold your little finger every now and then.

All the folks at the Cheshire Home say they miss you. You have been looking after the residents for so many years, unwavering in your care and support. Even though you had retired from nursing, you could not keep away from your passion, nursing. You still continued to work at the Cheshire Home, and made it your second home. It is hard to imagine that just four months ago, you were still going to work and everything was well.

It is a testament to the kind of teacher and colleague you were that so many of your young nurses from those days, even till now, have become your "adopted daughters". I have had to share you with so many "siblings" this way, though I never minded. You are the most generous person I know, generous with your laugh, your jokes, your time for people in trouble, for friends seeking counsel.

I remember the times I would come home and you would be on the phone counselling someone. Or we would have a guest and you would be advising him or her. You even let a porter, whom you met in England on one of your travels, stay with us when he visited Singapore. I have followed suit. Remember the two brothers from Cyprus who came to stay with us? I had also met them on a holiday and invited them to stay with us if they ever came to Singapore. You joked with them: "Please take my daughter's photo and show it to your friends and see if she can find a husband that way." That was why you called our home "Why not Homestay", remember? Because of the various friends you would invite to sleep over.

In the same vein, thank you for accepting all my friends too. You are a friend to all of them and, in fact, some of them have claimed you as their mother or godmother – this is you, not being selfish in how much you give and whom you give it to. My friend, Rex, says he remembers the first time he met you was after he had puked all over our floor from drinking too much. You had simply cleaned up after him and made him comfortable. That is the essence of you: No judgement, accepting people as they are.

For me, watching the direct impact you have made on people is what I will always hold dear. And it works both ways too, since everyone you have helped loves you back. You seem to do it, time and time again, without complaint. As I grow older, I realise these are precious lessons I have learned, consciously and subconsciously – how it is better to be big-hearted than hold back in helping others, whether it is giving money or a listening ear. Thank you for showing me what love is, what compassion is, for being the example of all I want to be – caring, loving and kind.

Even with your illness, you still put others as a priority. Last Christmas, tired and unwell as you were, you insisted on going to see your neighbours and giving the children *angpow* and gifts. And you wanted to return home from the hospital because you were still thinking of us and making sure we are looked after should anything happen to you. But it is our turn to look after you now, Mummy.

Mummy, thank you for your many sacrifices over the years, how you had to work different shifts to provide for us, riding bus 166 from our place to the Singapore General Hospital early in the morning, and rushing home to cook our favourite fish curry or stew (with extra potatoes) or *tau yu* (soya sauce) chicken.

Thank you for inspiring me with your work ethic. No complaints, no presumptions; just simply getting up and going to work, shift after shift, sometimes with little rest or sleep in-between. Through your example, you have shown me how we should approach life – naturally, going with the flow, enjoying the moments along the way.

In the words of American writer Max Ehrmann from his poem, "Desiderata", which you made us memorise:

> Go placidly amid the noise and haste and remember what peace there may be in silence. As far as possible, without surrender, be on good terms with all persons. Speak your truth quietly and clearly and listen to others, even the dull and ignorant; they too have their story.

These words still ring true and clear, etched in our memories, a wonderful point of reference about what it means to be loving and caring.

There are so many things over the years, Mummy, for which I have not thanked you enough. Thank you for being with me throughout my pregnancy and being with Aleia, my dearest daughter, our gift. I am so happy to be a mother myself now, and she is just four months old. I am thankful for the time you have spent with her. I will always remember our first visit to the pediatrician and how you carried her during our taxi ride. How you looked after her even when you yourself needed looking after. How you helped me in the middle of the night during those first few weeks, and all the little tips you had given on how to look after her.

Thank you for all the celebrations – the Christmas parties, the chicken paratel, the *masak merah*, and more, that you cooked for my friends and colleagues. Thank you for making us feel special and making a big fuss on our birthdays. It is always a celebration in our family, never forgotten, definitely with gifts and nice *makan*.

Thank you for being at all my graduation ceremonies and again, making a fuss about them, particularly in the photo taking. Even though we might grumble when you asked us to pose, you would rush to make copies when the photos were out. And you take the best photos! Even when my friends had already engaged photographers for their weddings, they would ask you to take photos too, because you could capture the best smiles and poses!

Thank you for taking us with you wherever you went when we were younger. For instance, going to Poh Heng, where we used to love sitting on the bar stools in the jewellery shop as the staff brought out different pendants and chains for us to look at. But we were more interested in the soft drinks he gave us, Sinalco! But you had the patience to share stories with him, eventually buying beautiful little trinkets, like the jingly Nona charm bracelet which I still wear.

We also loved shopping along High Street – for a special Christmas dress or frock, with matching shoes, and having Polar Café curry puffs afterwards. We used to visit the

Wonderland amusement park, with its big Ferris wheel; riding in a double-decker bus (how exciting that was for the first time!); the movies (even the *Dracula* films we watched at Paramount cinema in Serangoon Gardens); going to the hairdressers or facials at Aunty Sally's; the tailors (poring over the maxis, midis and fashion books); People's Park (buying material and eating chicken rice after, although we loved the one at Swee Kee too). What beautiful memories you have given us, Mummy.

Thank you, too, for the holidays, all the trips to Penang, spending Christmases with cousins, and that very special trip to the US.

Thank you for paving the way for my relationship with God. Thank you for taking us to church and making sure we knew God early so that we could develop our own special relationship with Him. I shall give Aleia the same opportunity and hope she discovers herself how special this can be.

Thank you for all the love, laughter, joy, tears, lessons, warmth and hugs; thank you for letting us be *bo tua bo sway* (not respecting elders) with you.

Thank you for the wonderful relationship I have shared with you. You are not only my mother but also my friend, confidant, counsellor, teacher and *kay poh* (busybody) number 1. This relationship has encouraged me to be more open with you, talk freely with you and share my opinions.

I love you, Mummy.

Dr Rose (extreme right) wih her sister Sheela Ann Demel and their mother Ruby Rudra, Christmas 1999.

Dr Rose Marie Sivam leads the team at Pantheon Media, a media consultancy. She has produced programmes for international broadcasters such as Channel 4 (UK), ARD (Germany), BBC International and ASTRO. She has also worked with the UN to drive the Eco4theWorld project, an environment-inspired global initiative. Dr. Sivam and her husband, Chef Chris Choo of Relish.Sg, host *My Home Your Home*, inviting guests to share a meal with people from all walks of life, an initiative commended by Singapore's Deputy Prime Minister Heng Swee Keat during his Budget Speech in 2019.

Joy. Luck. Club

Georgette Yu

Ma, you welcomed me into this world at the young age of 26 – a lucky number – and you were on your way to be a mother of two. Then two became three and then, we are four.

Twenty-six is also the number of years I had left Manila. I was then a stranger to Singapore, this place I now call home. Twenty-six years later, whenever I return to Manila, I am the stranger back home.

Each year, the birthdays will come and go, with not much to toast about. As time passes, the dates slowly fade from your memory. You asked me once, with a confused frown: "Why is it harder to remember?" I replied: "It is okay."

It is okay, Ma. I remember. I have found that my stories are buried deep in your stories. Things have changed, people have changed. I thought I have changed. But I have not – I was then, and still am, your daughter. And here, I remember our past.

Joy

I recall, as clear as daylight, I was six and furious. You did everything right as what my teacher had asked. You had bought me an apron with pockets. Proudly, I wore it on stage as I danced to carefully choreographed steps in front of beaming parents.

I had red apples in my pockets – but not for long. The next moment, I scrambled around the stage, chasing, not one, but two red things rolling on the stage. Two apples that simply refused to go back into my pockets. I think the audience laughed, and I was sad.

You came to pick me up after the performance. I did not say a word but was filled with anger. Did you not think it through when you got me that little apron with two tiny pockets? I told you the apples had dropped. You nodded; I swallowed my disappointment. Then you held my hand and we walked home.

***

You called my name: "Georgette, Georgette, Georgette." Your voice was calm, yet determined. You stirred me awake with an urgent tug on my shoulder. It was dark but the neighbour's roosters were already crowing. Aaah! Why do you have to wake me up at this hour! But you left before I could say a word and went about the routine of a typical school day.

Our family was crammed into a small bedroom. Dad was still sleeping. Geoff got up and so did I, with eyes half-closed. A pail of water and a face towel to wash two tiny faces and open up our tiny eyelids. School uniforms were ready and so were bowls of oatmeal on the vanity table, doubling up as a breakfast table for two.

Then I heard you scream: "GEOOOFF!" His body had gone limp. You held it tight, shook his head and called his name again. I looked on in fear. Chaos ensued. I was eight and afraid. The next thing I knew, I was off to school with Aunty Rosa. Left in school for the day, with my brother sick at home. I waited eagerly for school to end.

RIIIIIINNNNNGGG! The school bell rang. I quickly packed my books and drifted down the hall. I craned my neck and peered beyond the iron gates. On the other side, there were smiling faces, laughing faces, noises and chatter of parents and guardians.

On my side, there was some shoving and pushing, shouting and friendly goodbyes. Slowly, the shoves were still. Noises were quieter. Goodbyes were silent. My classmates left. Still, I waited behind the iron gates. Silence surrounded me as I listened intently to the ticking clock. Slowly, darkness fell; I thought you would not come. I contemplated on darkness.

You finally came; I lifted myself up. You held my hand and we walked home.

But this day had taught me the feeling of loneliness.

***

Do you remember our old house that overlooked the canal always filled with trash? Sometimes, I waited for a dead body to float up. Well, I have been reminiscing about that apartment, the rooms, our neighbours, and the street. I have been trying to recall the size of that apartment. How big was it? Everything seemed relative as I was tiny… and invincible.

Back then, you were mostly busy in the kitchen, preparing food and cooking with Aunty Rosa. It never seemed to end when you had to feed a battalion of extended family members as the long table awaited the meal to be laid out. You accepted what you had to do and what it means to be a daughter-in-law. Being Mom sometimes had to take a back seat.

Over time, I watched you steer your youth through marriage and motherhood with such filial piety worthy of a telenovela. You are the protagonist who brings happiness and joy, because Ah Ma had changed your Chinese name to *Le Le* (joy). This is when your story takes an ironic turn.

On good days, you could spend your precious time with us nonchalantly. Remember when you showed me how to prepare snacks using the toaster hidden from everyone else in our bedroom? We were sneaky and felt high and mighty as we ate up our mess.

However, on some days, you tried to stage a mutiny and fought hard on your own. These were the days when tables and chairs were overturned. You shouted and cried with frustration at being treated this way. Ah Ma was silent. Everyone was silent. The TV noise filled the void. I simply sat around, not knowing what to do.

The next day would unfold like any other; we would take walks together, cross that putrid, stinking canal as I held my breath and gripped your hand tightly, not wanting to let go of Joy.

Luck

I got your package from *Tua Yi* (Eldest Aunt). As instructed, I slipped on the white t-shirt for the night and the next day, pass it to her, who would then pass it back to you when she returned to Manila. This white tee was an odd addition to my wardrobe filled mostly with black clothes. Most significantly, the red, boldly painted script on its back felt like a pea hidden beneath the weave as I wore it uncomfortably to sleep.

Not surprisingly, my dear husband gave me a quizzical look, to which I responded with a killer stare enough to throw his questions off. He was unprepared for my peculiarities, including my obsession with cleanliness. But, let me address the elephant in the room.

My life has always had the supernatural.

***

Before I came across the book of Shakespeare's poems hidden in Pa's dusty shelves, I had started reading palms. We would travel to places on Jeepneys and meet palm readers in their tiny huts. They would stare at me and foretell, with glee, a blissful life but would lower their voices to warn me of my doom.

Ma, you would fork out a tidy sum, saved up from your meagre allowance. Some stories they told have stuck with me over the years, but others were not worth a penny. I was young then and their visions mesmerised me. My tiny palm revealed a future, and I crafted my own adventures. There are lines of life that flow, love gets entangled, and fortunes are missed.

In particular, there was a story told by a travelling couple that made you feel defeated. They foretold visions of my marriage past my prime, and possibly children, though not many. But lo and behold, the psychics then claimed they could transcend time to nullify the bad fortune. They had asked for a sum of money which was beyond reasonable; you asked to be given some time to consider it.

I was a teenager then and was fumbling my way through traditional gender roles. I enjoyed being the only girl in the family, but also wanted to have the same opportunities as my brothers to have a career. Being told I would have a late marriage and few children, I replied to you, was not a bad thought.

However, you frowned. You discussed with Pa, but there was no way to get that much money. Dejected, you let them go with your hope on hold. You wanted to change the course of my fortune; however, we did not reach a deal with fate.

My fate then moved offshore to Singapore. I was far and remote. What the fortune-teller said somehow came true: Life flows, fortune not amiss, but love got entangled. Pa was out of his wits. Geoff questioned my taste for men. You were quiet. Five years away from home and I came back with a bombshell: A middle-aged Caucasian man for a boyfriend.

Pa tried to reverse its course, but I fought him hard, maybe blinded by my feelings. I felt the concerns from everyone, but you never sat me down or talked your way through the grim situation. Only once you tried, and we were back with the clairvoyant, now with different tricks up her sleeve. This time, instead of palm, she fiddled with my toes.

Pressing them one by one, she waited, then another, and she raised her eyebrows. Maybe this toe, I offered. With curly hair and a stout body, she readjusted the low stool and repositioned her booty, like a cat ready to pounce. I told her I frequently practised yoga and perhaps the toes were flexible and not feeling arthritic to get the reactions she needed. She smiled. This time, there were no stories foretold; only sage advice to keep my eyes open for secrets not told. Again, you felt defeated.

As we enjoyed an afternoon alone together, you asked if I was hiding the pain from the clairvoyant. I said I was not hiding any physical pain. But truth be told, I have kept from you the pain that life has thrown at me; I live with insecurities, failures and betrayals. I have had to deal with them all. Life has served me punches that have hardened my soul but also hard enough to knock me down the road. We do not share comfort like other mothers and daughters, for the only comfort I get is not having your pain for my sorrows.

Ma, I went to see the palm readers and clairvoyants because you had believed in a better life for me and wanted to change the course of "unfortunate" events for me. I am a palm reader too. I have held your palm, read your life and seen the hardships you have had to endure. Your hands are rough, fingers crooked from toiling and a symbolic cheap metal ring you wear, bought from spare change you had, to better your own fortune. And I am a clairvoyant too. I have seen an image of you kneeling in front of the altar every morning with an incense stick and a prayer that lights up our souls – for me, for Pa, for my brothers and for everyone you hold dear. You pray for us each day, but never for yourself.

I will heed the sage advice to keep my eyes open for secrets not told. And this is my secret: My life has indeed been blessed by the supernatural, by your superhuman gift of love. Thank you, Ma.

Club

Twenty-six years ago, I arrived in Singapore with an emerald-green Delsey hardcase luggage that Pa had bought for me. With much difficulty, I lugged it along, me with my tiny frame and a huge suitcase heavy with belongings. They were things you had bought and packed for me, right after Pa had confirmed my one-way ticket out of Manila. It was my survival kit.

There were the Victorian floral-designe handkerchiefs that wiped away my tears; your bulky, thick cable sweater that gave me the warm fuzzy feeling; and a bright pink, palm-sized alarm clock that rang with intense warning. However, most of the things inside the suitcase have faded in my memories. What was once full of things that comforted me, I have since left them behind in my plight to fit into a new world.

Georgette (right) with her mother on holiday in Japan in 2019.

Twenty-six years have passed and this foreign land is now my home. In this new home, the bright pink alarm clock has long been tucked away, replaced by the digital phone. Yet, I still hear its soft ticking, reminding me of our moment together before I left, and my memories of you. At that time, perhaps you would have sensed my fear of leaving home. Would you have known that I might not come back home? Instead, you had shown me courage and allowed me space to lead my life in this new world.

The colour of my bright pink alarm clock has become dull. I hold it in my palm, wishing that I could travel back in time. To a time where I was still in your world. Your world where I was not judged, I was not faulted; where I did not doubt, I did not second-guess; where I did not feel wronged, I did not feel scorned. It was where I was flawed and imperfect but accepted as your daughter.

I remember, Ma, and I pray that everything will be okay.

Love,
Georgette

Georgette Yu is a freelance designer and a fashion lecturer with the Nanyang Academy of Fine Arts. She completed her Masters in Arts Pedagogy and Practice from Goldsmiths College in 2018. Her research work explores creativity and the identity of artist-educators.

11 Years

Zuraidah Mohamed

Have you ever lost someone you love and wanted one more conversation, one more chance to make up for the time when you thought they would be here forever? If so, then you know you can go your whole life collecting days, and none will outweigh the ones you wish you had back.

Mitch Albom,
For One More Day

Mama, it has been 11 years since you died and I remember that morning vividly still. It was five in the morning. I was working out at sea, hours away from home. I can still remember the events and the whole conversation that took place, word for word.

It was my colleague who broke the news to me. He asked first if I was all right and told me to have a seat. The sombre look on his face terrified me. I knew something was wrong but never would I have thought it would be something to do with you. He told me that someone at home had been trying to get hold of me for hours. That happened often because work took me to the middle of nowhere, where the network was quite scant. But the fact that someone from home was calling terrified me further. It was something that rarely happened and could only mean it was an emergency.

And then he told me: "I am so sorry. Your Mom passed away in her sleep." His words echoed in my head as I scrutinised my last moments with you.

It was some hours ago before I left for the night shift. You were your quiet usual self when I gave you a kiss on the cheek before I headed out. You were in bed as always, staring into space. I was trying to recall if I had missed anything. Any sign that would have indicated you were quietly leaving us. How could this have happened when you had no known critical illness? You were not sick. You just seemed to have lost the spark for life after *Abah*'s passing, that was all. I was barely through grieving over him and now, I would have to grieve you. Three months. That was how long I had just buried my father and here I was again, burying my mother. I know you had missed him terribly, Mama. I know he was the world to you. But he was mine too, and so were you.

The pain hit me the hardest the morning after your funeral. Waking up alone and remembering that *Abah*, and now you, were not there was such agony. This was the first day of my forever without the both of you. It was a morning marked by the smell of *bakhoor* (incense) that had been burning the night before, a smell that often took me back to old memories. It reminded me of the evenings when it was burned as a fragrance in my childhood home, of our prayer-cum-family gatherings, of family funerals. How bittersweet it was that this smell would remain forever as a memory of yours and *Abah*'s funerals.

I knew then how you had felt the morning after that fateful day, three months ago. I remember you were having breakfast in front of the TV in the living room. We had our meals there because that was where his bed was. He could not walk and had been bedridden for a long while. This was a spot where he could at least still see the comings and goings of the world outside, and of us when we came home. We would spend hours on the couch there, talking to him or watching TV together. You would occasionally nap there as well to keep him company. But that morning, after 35 years of being together, there you sat without him. You looked forlorn and lost.

Mama, I am sorry if I did not do enough for you then. It pained me to see you that way but I did not know what to do. All I could do was hug you. I wished I could have done more, because that was also the morning when you started slipping away from us. Because when *Abah* died, not only did he take your spark with him, he also took your will and spirit to carry on. The love you had from your children did not seem to be enough or equal to the love you had from him. You just could not find the reason to do anything anymore.

Soon, you became bedridden too, like *Abah*. It pained me to see you like that, letting yourself go when you were still blessed with mobility and some independence. I guess you found solidarity with him by suffering the same condition he had. I could see how much you were grieving for him in silence. No amount of encouragement from us could make you budge. That was also the last time we heard you speak.

You retreated into a world of silence and stayed that way until the day you took your last breath.

**

They say time heals. But nobody told me that the grief and pain does not end. There is no timeline or limit for it. As the years go by, it becomes more of a dull ache. But it can still come back in stinging waves. I guess your death was harder for me to accept because you had left us suddenly. Whereas *Abah* had been in the hospital for almost a month and we had already been told to be prepared for the worst. We managed to say our goodbyes when he was still lucid and conscious. I was also there when he took his last breath. But you slipped away quietly in your sleep. There were no goodbyes, no last words.

It has been 11 years, but I still feel your absence. On some days, it makes me smile. It comes through little things, moments and memories. Little things like a Cadbury's milk chocolate bar. I remember your love for it and how you would always have a block stocked in the fridge. There was once when I had made you so mad because I had finished the last piece of that block. Now, just like you, I always have chocolate stashed in my fridge.

But there are times when your absence still hits me hard. Milestones like birthdays, graduation, marriage and pregnancies. It has also crept up during the most surprising moments and situations, like during an activity in a course that I had to attend. It was a mandatory marriage preparation course and we were required to list the likes and qualities of our soon-to-be parents-in-law. My husband's answer was heartbreaking. He wrote that he would never get the chance to get to know you and *Abah*. He only hoped that he was someone the both of you would have approved of. At that point, your deaths had just passed their one-year mark. But the gravity of his answer and the reality of a future where neither of you were going to be in it, split open the wounds of my heart.

You would never be at the bride's table at my wedding. I would never get to learn the lessons of motherhood from you. You would never get to see the grandchildren that you had yearned for. Most of all, you would never get to meet my husband. You had seen and lived through the consequences of my bad relationship choices in the past. As much as it broke your heart then, I know you had never stopped praying for my happiness and inner peace. I never got to thank you for that, Mama.

Mama, I wish you have had the chance to meet him. He makes sure that a smile and a hug is what I wake up to every morning. He loves me unconditionally, just like how *Abah* was with you. I know for sure you both would have gotten along well. He has a soft spot for old folks and loves putting a smile on their faces. I would give anything to see that toothless grin of yours again. You deserve that, after all the pain that I had put you through over the years. There are so many other things that you deserve, but I never got a chance to give them to you. Like the comfortable twilight years that I so wanted for you.

Taking care of you and *Abah* during your ailing years was not easy. There were times when the challenges brought me down to my knees and times when I cried myself to sleep, wondering if there was enough strength for us to pull through. Times when I had to forgo my wants just to make sure I could afford the things you both needed, like medicines, health checks and a roof over our heads. Times when I wondered if I could have given you more.

At one point, it took its toll on me, mentally and emotionally. There were moments that I regretted and things I wished I could have done better. Seeing you both fading away as ill health and old age ravaged you was not easy. It was especially hard for me to see this happen to you because all your life, you were deaf. And with your eyesight failing, it only made your world smaller and more confusing. It made you feel isolated. On days like these, I looked forward to seeing your face light up whenever I came back. Despite the hardships, I hope you knew, Mama, that neither of you were a burden to me. In fact, I feel blessed to have been able to take care of you and *Abah*, thankful that I got to be on that journey during the remaining half of your lives. I hope my best efforts were good enough for you.

The only regret that remains is not having the opportunity to fix the broken pieces between us. I wish I had time to make new memories with you, to make up for the painful ones I had given you in the past. Time for more hugs and to tell you that I love you more than you thought I did. I wish I had more time to make up for what we had lost when I was growing up in somebody else's care.

Most of my life, people often saw me as your sister's daughter. I know that must have hurt you. I know that for years, you lived with the notion that I was ashamed of you because you were deaf, or as you often put it back then:

"Not like the moms of the other kids." It was a pain that you visibly carried, to which I added in my moments of anger to spite you when I could not get my way as a child or an angst-filled teenager.

But you never stopped being my mother. You loved and forgave me, even when my words and actions had hurt you. I wished I had apologised and let you know that my anger had all come from a confused place, and a notion that I had been hurting myself too. All those years when I was being raised by your sister, I often wondered why you had left me with her. Why couldn't you be my mother all the time and not just for the weekends? Why I saw *Abah* more than I saw you? Why my cousins went back with their parents every day while I did not?

I thought I was not wanted and eventually got used to being "left behind". That was the reason why I did not want to return to you or *Abah*. It was not out of hate, nor had I forgotten who my parents were. It was because your sister's home was the only one I had ever known and was used to. Her home was where most of my life had been spent. Maybe you had felt that your sister would have been able to take better care of me, since she was already babysitting other kids. Maybe you felt she would have been able to devote more time to me than you ever could, because she was childless. These questions, like your absence, still pop up in my mind sometimes. I will never get the answers now or say all that is left unsaid. But I believe you had done it out of love and for my well-being. It was a painful sacrifice but one you had to make.

Mama, I hope you know how much you were loved. Not just by your children and family, but the people whose lives you had touched and left behind. I saw this on the day of your funeral. We did not have space in our little flat in the end for all the people who turned up. And they kept on coming even days after.

Your selflessness and strength were what most of them remembered you for, and I remember the same too. I learned about empathy and helping others by watching you. We were not well-to-do, but you often went out of your way for those who had lesser than we did. Like the blind man who came by our neighbourhood every weekend selling biscuits. You often bought a lot from him, even though I know you and *Abah* were struggling to make ends meet. I also heard how hard you had worked as a single mother to raise my half-brother after your divorce. This was before you met *Abah*.

Your life was never easy and full of adversities. You lived through the Japanese Occupation and experienced the racial riots during Singapore's early days. You had to grow up fast and with the rest of your siblings, help your mother when Abib left the family. But despite it all, your trust and belief in the goodness of others prevailed.

You often said that when it was your time to go, there was nothing much you could leave behind for us. But you did. It is the legacy of your kindness, which lives on in your children and the people whose lives you had touched. I hope we have done justice to that legacy and your memory.

Eleven years. Eleven is a significant number for me. That was the date I got married: The 11th day of the 11th month in 2011. What a coincidence the timing of this letter; it would have been 11 years since you left us.

I will end this letter with a final goodbye and the words I never got to say enough when you were alive. Thank you, Mama, for everything. I love you so much.

Zuraidah in the arms of her mother, 1982.

Zuraidah Mohamed has a Bachelor's degree in Journalism and Communications Media Studies from Murdoch University. She is currently a freelance fixer for a Japanese newspaper. Zuraidah's articles have been published in several lifestyle websites. She has also volunteered her writing and photography skills to a local NGO, a private animal shelter and rescuer, creating write-ups and visual stories for their charity events.

Mother's Mother Tongue

Gwee Li Sui

Dear Mummy,

How precious words are between us and also how pointless! Even this word "Mummy", which Li Choo and I use to call you, could not have been yours. It was probably instilled in us by Papa, and our young selves misremembered it as originating with you. Papa has a few names: He was "Daddy" before he became "Dad" formally and "Papa" casually. You are always just "Mummy".

Today, as I sit at my writing desk, I find myself caught in this inconsequential oddity. It must be the first time in my half-century wondering why we call you by a single word. I am also wondering now why I did not wonder about this earlier. Why did Li Choo and I never evolve your name as we did for Papa or at least give you more names?

"Mummy" is strange because, in the Teochew you speak, the term of endearment should be *Ah Mak*. Yet that form never took root in our conversations as the way to call you or to mean you. We prefer *Ah Mak* to be for identifying others, as with *yee gai ah mak*, his or her mother, or *kia piak gai ah mak*, mother next door. "Mummy" is distinct. It is personal and, in our domestic Teochew, cosier than a proper word. When used on its own, it is simply you.

How remarkable! Am I just realising the implication? "Mummy" is the only English word you have let slip into your everyday life. It is the only foreign word you have allowed to puncture your reality, which, in all our years, has remained unspoilt by the cacophony of languages around us. There was the Malay of kampong life, and there is Papa's English. There is the Mandarin Li Choo and I started bringing home from school one day, which has since filled your every waking hour through that perennial deaf rambler, the TV.

None of these has gained a foothold into the mind of your Teochew. They are mere birdsongs, rustling of trees, sounds of busy traffic. If language channels consciousness, if we dream in images but make the world with words, the way your world exists has stayed unmolested. "Mummy" is an entry point that opens and shuts at once. It belongs strictly to Papa, Li Choo, and me – and it is the sole otherly, motherly word you accept.

Admittedly, speaking to you has not been easy all this while. If it appears otherwise to passing observers, it is because I have gotten used to the effort required. Every line is always created over-consciously. Li Choo and I did not have that broad environment in Teochew, that network of native speakers, which you and Papa shared well into your adulthood. What she, being older, was able to gather fortuitously, I gathered less.

Both we, paper Hokkiens, were born into Teochew – and then Papa felt the urgency to ground us in his centrifugal English. School education subsequently took over this mission of tying us to a larger social body in which we ought to operate for the rest of our lives. Our lessons in Teochew were officially over. Neither of us has advanced since.

My Teochew remains a 10-year-old's Teochew. My small vocabulary is used to speak with you in the way a Swiss army knife is used to cook meals in the wild. Every word strains at its variety of uses and abuses in my staccato mouth. I begin a sentence and often find myself midway gazing into a dark room, unsure where to go for what I need. It is like missing a step and falling into a manhole. I grasp at thin air. The seconds expand. I turn to Papa or Li Choo with pleading eyes – they shrug their shoulders.

Because you cannot learn my words, I grope around for yours. When nobody is able to help or when nobody else is present, we fashion our own means to meet. Mother and Son retool a tongue to fill the sudden gaps. I stutter in Mandarin – and, when you understand, you nod and talk on. When even Mandarin fails, I resort, with little expectation, to English. On your part, you speak in rudimentary Teochew unhurriedly.

You express with a gentleness I still cannot graft onto my daily English. I recall the same quality in the Teochew of Ah Ma, who, hunchbacked as you are now, spoke musically as if to measure time rather than to crowd it. Your speech, too, flows like a soft radio song whose words are caught while stirring from daydream. It dances with hope and innocence and waits for company.

I have learnt very early this difference between not knowing another language and being unable to speak anything else. Most people cannot tell them apart because often, their opposites occur together. When someone picks up a new language, say, German or Thai, he or she has also acquired that language. Few suspect that, in fact, two things are gained: Another language and the ability to acquire languages.

To learn a language presumes an ability to acquire. This ability comes first – or how could what was taught come together to be learnt? I think that you lack this ability to acquire languages. In all our years, I cannot get you to say "orange juice"; you say *oleng ju*. I cannot teach you to say *roti prata*; you keep repeating *loti paranta*. What is not Teochew – regardless of how many times you have heard it – rolls off your tongue with its own sound. You make up words; you are always making up words. I struggle to recognise what you mean and then make do with what you offer as words.

When I was small, I asked you many times why you could not speak or read even a little Mandarin, Malay, or English. I asked you to learn with me, our age difference aside, but you replied that you could not. I failed to understand then. I played with your long, black pigtail once, using its end to brush your cheeks and tickle your lips. You explained how you never learnt in a formal way. Education stopped too soon after it began. Your family needed your help at home. You were the 7th of 10 children.

Your lost education never reached Li Choo and me with regret. You described it with warmth and relief, putting in us our first impression of fidelity and modesty. Something had to be done, someone needed to do it, and you stepped up.

The times expected men and women to fulfil vastly unlike roles for the family, the kampong, and society. While you could not be more to yourself, yet you are only all of yourself. That, too, is freedom. You were very eloquent at a time when you and your children knew mainly Teochew.

Papa had a longer schooling than you and, in the few years more, mastered the Queen's English or the basics of it. He could recite Shakespeare, read pulp novels, enjoy Hollywood films; in the bathroom, he used to croon like Cliff Richard. His mornings would begin with *The Straits Times*, which he subscribed and dutifully read for decades – until he lost interest in this restless world.

Like you, Papa eventually left school to help support his family. He found a good clerical job in the civil service, and it firmed up his place in an otherwise intimidating Big World. He was effectively trilingual – although Malay soon dropped out from underuse. But it was in neither English nor Malay that he wooed you, was it? It could not have been. All of us bend to your world because it cannot change.

Our pliancy might be part of the problem or *the* problem – we do not dare think. It helped turn your inadequacy into a stronghold, strengthening your kingdom. You became the centre that, to this day, stops us three from drifting into other universes. Papa, like you, does not speak Mandarin. Your children speak English and Mandarin but with conflicting levels of competence. You need not struggle. You, who are illiterate, are the sole custodian of binding communication.

You, in our home, are the heart of our lives. Your job description as housewife – to clean, to mop, to wash, to cook, to look after us kids – is conveniently wordless. You took quickly to a routine that left you abundant time to spend with "friends": The dialect-based Rediffusion, the TV images, relatives on the phone, neighbours at the gate.

You claim how, at one stage, before my schooling began, I had been a handful. Those stories you still tell are vague to me, but the only one I do recall, you do not retell. It was about the day when I, throwing a tantrum at the foot of Mazu's altar, caught you at a bad time. You were cooking and apparently stressed by adult thoughts I had no access to. Tired and annoyed, you screamed at me and batted me with the flat steel of the chopper in your hand – shocking me so much that I dashed out of home.

As I ran, I made up my mind never to return. I felt that I lost your love. I had nowhere to go and would be homeless; plans whirled with each quickening step. But I did not get very far because, at the void deck of our block, you found me. We were both wet on our cheeks as you talked me into going home together. What did you say to me in Teochew then? This was my single memory of running away.

What is my mother tongue? In my formative years, I had been taught to call English my "first language" and Mandarin my "second language". All Singaporeans speak English and then Mandarin, Malay, or Tamil, after our respective ethnicity. I did not think much about how contrived that sounded. I repeated the notion as part of what gave me clarity and pride as a child of a young nation. It made sense also because I lived in an age with two realities: The official-speak and the reality.

Not until as late as my years as a doctoral student in London did this formation start to rattle hard. I found it immensely difficult to explain to anyone unfamiliar with

Singapore, my small world, and specifically, my mother tongue. Once, a Briton exclaimed in exasperation: "It should not be so difficult to answer. What *is* the language you spoke on your mother's lap?"

How was I to answer him? If I said Teochew, it would ring false since Teochew is not an official language of Singapore and I am not fluent in it. If I said English, it would still be inaccurate since I did not begin in English and the early form I embraced was, at best, Singlish. Mandarin and Cantonese do not even qualify since neither is my *mother's* tongue.

To make matters worse, I returned to a Singapore where some precarious scale had tilted at last. I now hear that Mandarin is my "mother tongue language" because I am ethnically Chinese and Chinese speak Mandarin. But these words – mother tongue, Mandarin, Chinese – are a juggler's balls in my head. They never met one another in the realities of my family. They were never clear; now they are telling me that they are truths.

My non-Chinese friends, weaned on this notion of Chineseness, cannot know my world. My Chinese friends, who have been eased into a new security, make little of my vexation. They treat Teochew lazily as like any so-called "dialect", a mere variant of Mandarin, forgetting how, even in basic speech, differences live large. Mandarin has one character for "Who?" but Teochew two: *Di diang?* Mandarin needs three characters to say "What is going on?" but Teochew two: *Zo ni?* Where is this equivalence? I fall again into the dark hole.

You and Papa are always in the world I have for myself in my creative works. Both of you began at the fore and recede into the values and composure. Papa was everywhere in my first published comic book, *Myth of the Stone*. He was the wise garuda Keagga, the jovial centaur Sashbun, wrathful Browgin the gryphon, nervous Crumblie the dwarf. He was the enigmatic Maudus Rex, Lord of the High Worlds. But you permeated my first poetry book, *Who Wants to Buy a Book of Poems?* Your Teochew breathed its rhythms, your levity held up its moods, your eyes looked out of its themes.

You came to the fore again during the AWARE Saga years ago, when a group of Christian conservatives hijacked a women's rights organisation. In the wee hours of that day of its climactic members' showdown, I could not sleep and sat down to write a poem. I thought simply of you, of what you would be doing. You would be setting out as usual for the ones you love, boiling water before we woke so that we could meet any day with warmth in our bellies.

I thought too of the three Marys who, on Easter morning, arrived at Jesus's tomb with embalming spices for his corpse. They did not know yet what had happened; they came not knowing. Are not these figures also you – enduring, loving, dutiful, and humane, celebrating life? You fell into my poem:

But Dawn is a woman.
In my parents' house, she wakes up first
to boil drinking water, a gentle presence
smelling of dew. She arrives first at the grave,
and she arrives again and then a third time.
She is that diurnal creature of hope, a face
opened to the sleeping day, willing to trust,
needing the fists of no man's ego,
lesser still, a hardened idea.

Li Sui and Mummy.

Mummy, this letter will not be read. It is not just because I write in a language you cannot read. In any other language, you will not be reading this. I, on the other hand, lack the real competence to bridge our languages, to translate it all into oral Teochew. My mother is illiterate and yet, without the full might of language, commands my universe. She deftly flaunts her moves to make us her planets as she blazes and rouses and gives us warmth.

Perhaps language is not this philosophical "house of being" or "flower of the mouth" after all. There are meanings that reside with words and are still untouched by them. Mummy, when we converse, you hear and treasure something other than my failure and I something other than your closure. In our laughter, we know that words are irrelevant. There is nothing here that I have not already said to you every time we are together. Yet I have not said it, and I need not.

Your Son always,
Li Sui

Gwee Li Sui has the happiest imaginable childhood and does not intend for it to end. This is why he became a writer because now he gets endless homework without the badgering of adults. He has seven volumes of poetry to date, the most recent being *This Floating World*. His other popular titles include *Spiaking Singlish: A Companion to How Singaporeans Communicate* and *The Leeter Tunku*, a Singlish translation of Antoine de Saint-Exupéry's *The Little Prince*.

Don't Hedge Your Bets

Wahid Al Mamun

Dear Ma,

The first time you actually listened to me read my poetry out loud was in 2017. I had somehow managed to bluff my way into a reading for young poets at the Singapore Writers Festival, and had a five-minute slot at the Festival Bookstore.

I do not remember being too nervous, but throughout the reading I could not help but look for you in the crowd. You had an inscrutable expression that threatened to throw me off. I think you knew the poems were going to be about you. But it must have been strange for you to be in the audience nonetheless.

Perhaps this is why I am so reluctant to show you my work. What if you do not like it? Even worse, what if you do? What if my poems are too true, what if they refashion the mother-son relationship through verse? What if the life of this relationship supersedes the real thing?

Still, afterward, I would ask you: "How did you like it?"

You would say: "You are a good writer." But you would mention nothing about liking or disliking my poems. Instead, you pick up your phone and say: "Let's find your father and go home."

That is why I always second-guess when I write poems about you. What does it mean to lay bare the intimacies of family life on paper? Is nothing above the desire for the reader to know, and to know voraciously? I think of Karl Ove Knausgård, the Norwegian author of the uncomfortably autobiographical *Min Kamp* series, who once remarked (to no less than his estranged ex-wife) that he felt like his writing entailed a Faustian bargain, where he deemed his books and his art to be more important than a functional relationship with his family. Or another Norwegian author, Vigdis Hjorth, whose semi-autobiographical *Will and Testament* led her mother to sue her. It also led to her sister writing a counter-novel where a woman bears the brunt of criticism from her narcissistic sibling's dishonest autobiographical novel.

Not that this will stoop to the same level of family drama. But sometimes, you ask me about when my first collection will come out, and I always give some noncommittal response. Soon. By the time I graduate. Maybe after I graduate. I do not know how or when to tell you that the more I think about a collection of the sort of poems I have been writing, the less I want it to see the light of day.

At some level, I am sure you understand. Once upon a time, you were a good writer. No – you are a writer. Because what is "once upon a time", if not an erasure dressed up as a fairy tale? You translate postcolonial African writers into Bengali and you write essays about the 1971 Liberation War and you write your speeches and sermons. You weave stories of your childhood with the present. You go on tangents mid-conversation that traverse time and geography and end up here, back home.

You often tell me how I remind you of my grandfather. Sometimes, you tell me the story of how, in 1971, he walked out of your house and sat down in a paddy field for three weeks to evade capture from the Pakistani army. I do not know how true this is but it does not matter – the rules of narratives need not adhere closely to fact. You set up risks and escalation, then climax and dénouement. And that is all I needed. Above all, you do what the very best of autobiographies sets out to achieve – you raconteur, you embellish, you captivate.

Sometimes, people ask me: "How did you become a writer?" To which I usually say: "How could I not?"

***

Once upon a time, there was a girl who lived in a small town in a country where nothing much happened. She was the 4th out of five children, so was neglected the way middle children tend to be. So the girl kept diary after diary that she filled out with imaginary friends and stories about faraway countries and resplendent futures that she could only dream about. She hid a transmitter underneath her pillow so she could listen to BBC radio plays in the middle of the night, with the volume cranked down as low as possible and her ear pressed against the speaker, so her grandfather would never find out. Her father found out, but told her to keep on writing. So she wrote and wrote and wrote until her teachers noticed her gift for writing; she wrote fairy tales in her board examinations and topped not only her town, but the entire state. The girl thought, rightly so, that she was destined for greater things.

Once upon a time, the girl realised she had to stoop to walk through the doorframes in her house.

***

In Chicago, the cold fronts shrivel my writing. I surprise everyone, including myself, and declare my major in Anthropology instead of English, as you had done all those years ago. I wish I can tell you why my writing has stagnated. Maybe it was the expectation of feeling like I had to settle into a place before I could write about it. More likely, it was the slow realisation that I was one drop of achievement in an ocean of overachievement. Here, I meet poets who coax blossom from white space, who whip a storm from a line break in ways I could only dream of. Over time, I gain a sinking feeling that I have no stories of note to tell in Chicago, because what is a story if not told excellently? Perhaps that left turn into Anthropology makes more sense now. At least in Anthropology you can bend your self-doubt into self-reflexivity.

Already, I can hear your counterargument – it does not matter how good other people are. You just have to keep on writing. You have to believe. I can only think: How do you back a losing horse so insistently?

Or, to be more precise, how do you back a losing horse who gave you a haemorrhage the moment he was sliced out of your belly? How do you back a losing horse who took you away from your life? How do you back a losing horse who, instead of finding a second wind and running to the front of the pack, writes about you in a bunch of poems that never really amount to anything?

Perhaps this is what motherhood is – maybe motherhood is couched in the regardless. Sometimes, you look at me and say: "One day, you will have children of your own. Then you will understand."

I would not know what it means to "understand". But the enigma is powerful enough to leave a worm buried deep in my mind.

***

Once upon a time, the girl grew out of girlhood and moved to the big university in the capital, where she read Shakespeare and debated Marx and played table tennis and marched against the military government and ended up in the cover story of the national papers. She landed a high-ranking job in the foreign office straight out of university and fell in love with a quiet man who needed her to stamp a student visa for Australia. As though struck by inspiration, she decided to pursue a graduate degree in Norwich, where she met friends from Italy and Greece and Ethiopia and Trinidad and Tobago. She wrote letters to the quiet man, who finished his Masters in Perth and started looking for jobs elsewhere. The world seemed so big and so blue and the girl was perpetually in awe that it kept on spinning out a fresh day every day.

***

It is December 2019. I am sat in my great-aunt's house in Surrey, just outside London. I have not seen my great-aunt since I was seven. When people meet our family, they say that you and I are the extroverts of the house. Wait till they meet Saju Nanu. Every time I talk to her on the phone, Saju Nanu will have ready a childhood anecdote, a verse from the *Qur'an*, and a quip from the latest feminist panel she attended at the ripe old age of 81. Perhaps this is where the family's storytelling gene comes from.

Despite the 14 years since my last visit, Saju Nanu is still quick to recognise me when I arrive at her doorstep. Before I even manage to walk through the doorframe, she tells me how you used to come here too, more than 30 years ago when you were a graduate student in Norwich. You would take the three-hour train out to London and spend an afternoon with her. She pulls out a neat binder of letters and correspondences with you that she has kept since the 90s. I am struck by the insistent regularity of these letters, how your handwriting has always looped about itself and taken up so much space on the page. Over time, of course, these correspondences moved online, and yet here they were in their physical fact, printed and compiled in the binder.

There is something so old-fashioned about writing to keep in touch, to sit in front of paper and to deliberate your thoughts exclusively for a person halfway around the world. As I flip through the binder, I think of the constancies of movement and recursions of movement in our family, as imagined through writing. Here I am, sat on the exact same settee that you sat on all those years ago, in the exact same sitting room with the exact same ochre wallpaper.

I feel weighed down by a strange sense of predestination. Maybe there is a template for how the rest of my life will turn out.

Towards the bottom of the binder, I find an email from early 2018, which you had sent Saju Nanu my poems from the reading. You say: "I do not really agree with everything he writes but it is not my position to agree. I am just glad he is writing."

***

Eventually, the quiet man came back and said he loved her back. He said: "Have you heard of a place called Singapore?" And she thought of her stories of faraway places from when she was a girl and thought: How wonderful, to be in love with a dreamer. And then she married the quiet man and left her diaries behind and settled down in a foreign place to become a teacher.

This is where I would normally write, the end. Except it isn't. It is not even the beginning. Because once upon a time far more recent than once upon a time, the girl woke up and found, to her shock, an angry cut on her belly and grey hairs on her pillow. She realised she had no friends in Singapore and her father was long dead and the quiet man has moved into another room in the house, with his dreams. And not a single diary to her name. Outside, the days are flat and sticks to the windows, like fruit-flies.

***

It is January 2021 and to my own disbelief, I find myself on a transatlantic plane back home. An unexpected surgery for my father has put everything else on hold. To while away the time, I reread Rachel Cusk's *Outline*. On parenthood, she writes:

I'm afraid you're mistaken in thinking you're that important. Children leave or children stay depending on their ambitions: their lives are their own…and besides, why should [children] be perfect? It is our own idea of perfection that plagues us, and is rooted in our own desires.

It is truly a bewilderment of our society that it sets up the nuclear family as a functional, contiguous unit, right until the point children hit adulthood. All of a sudden, these children stop being children and are foisted with a magical sense of independence and ambition. Isn't there great rupture there, isn't there a profound breakage when Cusk says that "their lives are their own"? What is parenthood, then, but a gaping lack?

It is strange to think of all this. Stranger still, when I am hurtling over the oceans back to square one. As though all of what Cusk said was suddenly undone by this fact. Like a writer balling their draft up and starting on a fresh page once more.

At the end of the day, what does it mean to be objective when writing about you? I do not want controversy, but I want dishonesty even less. Maybe this is why my writing has shrivelled up into its husk. Because I am afraid of committing to extending beyond admiration when I write about you. Because when I look beyond this sheen that I have carefully assembled in my poetry, I see only the emptiness of a life shorn of potential.

Strangely, I find it easy to locate myself at the centre of this crime, as though things would have worked out better for you, things would be better with my father if I had not come into this world. Would I have to write about the marriage? Would I have to write about the way your days stretch out into vacancy when my father is at work and when both your sons are on the other side of the world?

***

My favourite poem about you is, in fact, not about you at all. At a museum in Melbourne, I saw a mother in a cable-knit sweater and a beret patiently bring her toddler around the Impressionist gallery. There was something so sublime about the moment that I could not quite shrug off. It was also one of the last times I had felt true, spontaneous euphoria while writing a piece.

I do not think I will share the full piece with you, not just yet. Although there is a line that keeps on coming back to me – "the first act of love is a breakage". Which is to say that I believe there is something so violent about love. I am sure you understand. There is a scar on your belly that tells you as much. If motherhood is found in the regardless, then surely love is, too.

Perhaps there is a beautiful irony buried in all this – to figure this out about you, I had to write about someone other than you.

This is not to say that the poetry will come back, now or soon or ever, even. But maybe the point is not to think about collections, or about a career, or to find a way to freeze a living relationship into text. That would be impossible – there is still so much I have to say to you, so much I have left unsaid, so much that neither this letter nor a thousand poems could ever

Wahid with his mother in 2019.

get to the bottom of. And maybe that is something I will have to get better at living with.

    Perhaps all this is just an indirect way of telling you I love you, from one layer of remove. Sometimes I think of how I do not tell you this enough, in its bald fact. I do not tell you how insistently this emotion floats back to the surface, and maybe this is what I am hiding from. Perhaps I will have to find this solace once more. And I wish you the same grace in writing and in language, the way that you have always done since you were little.

Love,
Wahid

Wahid Al Mamun is a Singaporean of Bangladeshi origin currently studying at the University of Chicago, majoring in Anthropology with a minor in Creative Writing. His poem, "my mother thinks i dream in bengali", received an honorable mention in the Sing Lit Station's inaugural Hawker Prize for Southeast Asian Poetry in 2018. He has been featured in writers festivals in Singapore and Melbourne, and his works and translations have also appeared in the anthologies such as *Food Republic*, *Call and Response* and numerous *SingPoWriMo (Singapore Poetry Writing Month)*, as well as literary journal *QLRS*. At present, Wahid is on a one-man vendetta against string cheese.

Now and Always

Jean Tan

Dear Mom,

I turn 35 this year. It sounds like a really mature age to be. You already had two children by 35, while I still spend too much time on Netflix.

But it is hard to imagine how things could be any different. I had regained the ability to live normally only a short two years ago; for a significant part of my 20s, we had spent so much time waging war against kidney disease (mine). My 30s now seem like a breath of fresh air, finally free from health or relational crises that were the theme of the past three decades.

It does seem odd to be going on this new adventure of my life now without you next to me. Especially when we were soldiering through the trenches so closely together, and for so long.

I wish I were rich enough to buy us a large house, or two apartments next to each other, so that you would continue to be near me even as we keep our own spaces. But we know the cost of real estate in Singapore, perhaps more so than in dollars. For someone who had given her life to all her three children, especially as a single mom, 2020 was a heartbreaking year for you to see your last child leave. I know that it hurts deeply to be living alone, and you have been trying to cope with it as best as you can.

I do miss you. A lot, sometimes. But the strange thing is because we were so closely shouldering life together, being apart actually helps our relationship grow better now. It was no secret that my birth was a shock to you, and later, a heavy weight. You would recount the seemingly smooth pregnancy, the first greeting of the doctor – "Oh. It is okay, it can be mended" – and the hurrying away of the child even before you could hold her. The discovery of a severe cleft palate and clip, and then a succession of surgeries: At three months, one, and then nine, 16, 17, 18 years old. You shared about the years of despair, the sight of a child just out of the operating theatre, face bloodied and voice hoarse; the times you had to feed me one small spoonful at a time, and one hour for each feed, because the deformities meant I could not latch as a baby. You would recount, in desolation, the escapism of a husband who did not know what to do, and the marriage that slowly dissolved after my birth.

I still continue to grieve each time I recall your expressions of sorrow: Living often felt heavy, because my life was sustained at too great a cost.

But you did not stop at just feeding; you nourished me so completely. You instilled in me a love for stories and humour; you used games and puzzles to make me think. You invented and innovated, using candles and straws to train my lip and palate muscles – lighting the candle as I blew each flame out – and role-playing the characters in each book purposefully so I would respond in speech. You were the perfect speech therapist for me, devising a programme at home for me to practise consonants and vowels and sounds (how I struggled with the e's and s's), flicking the side of my cheek gently each time I slurred so I would repeat the words until I was clear enough to be understood.

And you did your best to create a loving, nurturing environment for me to grow up in. It might have been your professional training as an educator, or the natural spirit of learning and love for the arts that you carried. Either way, I remembered Beethoven, Norah Jones, and Taiwanese indigenous music playing in the house through my growing years; the piano with its particularly heavy keys we used to train strength; the lullabies we would sing together to make Brother sleep. Recently, I took a hot shower in the cold rainy weather and the song "小白船" (Little White Boat) came to mind most instinctively in that moment of "comfort" – my fave of the lot you sang us to sleep with. It was some years later, when I was older, that you told me about fighting in court to keep my piano lesson fees within the alimony. You told the judge, in tears: That "this child needs something on which to build her confidence".

Life was not always tough for us, though. Oh, the hours we spent shopping – I twirled around the mannequins as a young girl, waiting for you outside fitting rooms; as an older teen, I prowled the cheap malls looking desperately for festive clothes while you offered great advice on colours and style. We had interesting conversations about dating, politics, news events and skincare. You were such a good conversationalist, because you knew so much. Recently, we have shared a common interest in psychology, and the process of expanding new realms of knowledge together has been truly enjoyable. I recall now how this has not always been the case; I had clammed up completely in my early teens while going through a maelstrom of identity issues, but opened up in my later years as I grew more confident in general. I realise now that this was one of the best decisions I have made in our relationship, because of the great conversations we have grown to have in the many years after.

Our relationship was a beautiful, and yet strange one, so utterly intertwined, and therein laid too, the propensity for a bleeding into one. We both felt it violently as we went through my kidney disease together. The shock from the diagnosis was palpable; we held our tears back until you had left the hospital ward, and then the long, dark night began. It was a ridiculous state of affairs, given that I had gone through multiple surgeries already in my earlier years, and we thought we would both be done with hospitals after I turned 18. What laid before us now was a long-drawn, confusing foray into the unknown, because this immune condition had no clear medical cause or resolution. Was I to have kidney failure by the age of 40 or 50, according to one scenario the doctor described? Unfathomable – I was only 24. You were 56. It was not a strong age to be a caregiver all over again.

This ordeal felt a thousand times more difficult than the one before. Possibly because I was too young to remember the early stages of going through cleft surgery. Very likely too, because, unlike the foreseeable end to the cleft surgeries, this one was interminable and uncertain.

But in part, too, going through the kidney disease was difficult because we now had two strong-willed adults involved in the recovery process.

You were the same dedicated mother who researched extensively about the condition and its array of alternative treatments, cooking up a nutritional plan for me to strengthen the kidneys as much as possible. You worked on supplementation and religiously enforced a diet spanning from natural foods to herb infusions to juicing. You prayed fervently and wholeheartedly, tried to cheer me up with songs, and documented the ups and downs of the condition in great detail – to the detriment of your own eyesight and mental state.

But we were distraught and clueless when we realised the medications, nutritional plan, and alternative treatments could not sustain recovery, and relapse took place relentlessly, time and again – along with the repeated bouts of hospitalisations, proteinuria, swelling, puking, and chaos that took place in my internal system. We only realise, on hindsight, that it was just for seven years; when we both went through the battle on a yearly basis, each dragging on into another, it felt like there was no end.

I was too weak half the time, so I depended as much as I could on your regime. After a while, however, I struggled with eating foods that felt the same as my puke, and with going on a restricted lifestyle resulting in curtailing most of my social activities. It was no longer physical, but psychological – the extreme deprivation of sensorial good and social interactions drove me to borderline depression, and I began challenging the recovery regime. It was a hard war; we fought a lot, and this was the first time in our relationship we would scream repeatedly at each other. Poor Brother was caught up so much in it, and I am thankful for his sweet, patient disposition that helped us make peace each time.

But these battles continued – no longer just us fighting against the illness, but you and I, fighting each other. I began to lose heart; so did you. In our valiant attempt to overcome a long-drawn war, we had become bruised and beaten, sometimes by each other's words, and sometimes by our silences.

Somewhere along the way, I realised two things. The first was that if I wanted to get well, the responsibility had to be fully mine. Unlike in the first ordeal, which you shepherded in my growing years, I had to drive my own process of recovery now. Second, I realised that the ups and downs of the condition closely mirrored the events, choices, and emotions of the everyday – relapses came from eating food that is not cooked well, going for a run, periods, and even going through periods of high emotional or relational strain. This meant that I could not depend on anyone to regulate my own life for me; I had to do it, and develop great sensitivity to my own internal and physical state.

In other words, both realisations meant that I had to determine life and healing on my own terms – but I took some time to learn how to do so. I wonder if that discovery and the gradual challenging of your methods also meant that I was slowly eking out my own space for adulthood – but in a way that slowly displaced you from being the main caregiver of my life. I wonder, too, if that had also led to a sense of loss you had felt towards the end.

Because this had given you meaning and purpose for more than 20 years since my birth. As a fiercely protective mother, you resolved to make sure that, no matter what life brought, I would be okay. It was the cry of a determined and self-sacrificial parent, and all the more so because you were fulfilling two roles in the family. Coming to terms with the fact that you gave your absolute all – similar to how you made sure I could speak and live as a young child with a cleft – and still could not lead me to recovery, must be incredibly painful. It was a slow, painstaking cutting of the umbilical cord that had tied us together since my birth, but also this gradual letting go that enabled me to overcome my own helplessness and reclaim authority over my life.

Eventually, somehow, the symptoms cleared. I grew more confident in navigating the chaos of my own body, and healing took place in mental and emotional ways. After the doctor recommended that last drug, I had not relapsed for more than three years. It was a startling turnaround, given that we had exhausted all lines of defence and medications prior, and were this close to adopting one drastic resort of a medical approach which involved triggering the death of most B-cells in the body (Thankfully, we did not need to get there.)

Things have been so different since. We have entered a sort of unreal, twilight zone where things are actually mostly okay. I have never experienced so much peace as I did in the last two years. I got married, moved out, and the doctor's reports continue to be positive.

But I am here, and you are there; and sometimes I am wondering how life continues to be for you. I wonder if your hip is getting better, if you are painting, or looking at the flowers in your little balcony garden. I wish sometimes that we could walk regularly to the shops downstairs again, and have a bowl of noodles with conversations about everything. And when we do see each other, even for a few hours, I try to make you as happy as you can be – through nice dinners, tasteful ice creams, and fun cooking sessions (food is our thing). Somehow, even our conversations have taken a different turn; they are richer, seasoned with history and love, and the interactions more heartfelt. I wonder, too, if it could be a matter of time before we live near enough to each other again.

We both have our imperfections and scars, but it was a perfectly crafted journey, upheld by a God who made us for each other. Thanks, Ma, for being the best mother I could ask for in this life. You were a blessing from heaven, and you carried your responsibilities so well and competently, that I could not have turned out the way I did if not for your selfless love and sacrifice over many years.

I pray that while this season was not quite one you had expected, it is nevertheless still the start of a new season – one in which you live for, dream for, and thrive for your own self, and not for others. I pray it will be one of purpose, love, and building of strength, and that the next decade will shine so brightly that it overwhelms the darkness of the years that came before. I hope we can travel the world again – hopefully before I have a kid in tow – and even if a kid comes along, that he or she will be one who adores Grandma

Jean (left) wih her mother.

to the fullest. I pray it will be a season of new experiences and fullness of joy; in a different way from before, but not any less rich. And I pray that you will receive in full all the love you first poured out on those around you, and through a special someone you deserve.

Thank you for being a gift to me, Ma, now and always. I love you forever.

Jean Tan is a singer-songwriter who has performed at the Southeast Asian Games, Singapore Night Festival, The Esplanade's All Things New and Come Together festivals, and Zandari Festa in Seoul, Korea. Born with a cleft palate and lip and later diagnosed with kidney disease at 24, Jean often weaves her experiences with pain and love into her music. Jean shares primarily to build connection with people across settings, and has performed at schools, community spaces, and for organisations such as World Vision, Relief Singapore, and Operation Smile.

My Mom, My World

Jo-Anne Lee

Dearest Mommy,

As I sit at my desk, immobile in a cast, my left ankle sprained due to a silly step accident, I am missing you, Mommy. I cannot visit you for a while until my leg has healed.

I am missing you so much, knowing that the pandemic had temporarily separated us during the circuit break. Ironically, now that we are allowed to freely visit each other, it is my foot that gets in the way! What a year 2020 has been.

At my age, I am most grateful you are still alive. Most of my girl pals have lost one or both their parents, largely due to old age or sickness. My dear sweet Mommy, you are now 84, with mild cognitive dissonance (also known as dementia) that has been stable the last 12 years. I wish I could have shown the many videos I have captured of you in this letter, videos that reveal your joyous spirit in spite of your memory loss.

You may be less chatty, more dependent now, but your love still shines through for each and every one of us. The child in you comes alive and that is the most endearing and loveliest part of it all. I so love your giggles and kooky sense of humour. That is something your illness cannot take away from you.

I love the way you wait for me outside the house, sitting on the rattan chair when you know I am coming to visit, and the beaming smile you give me on my arrival. I love your healthy appetite for food. The way you enjoy your meals – *rojak, mee siam, kway chap, apom bokwa*, chicken curry, shepherd's pie, *kueh pie tee, popiah, keropok* (whether it is prawn, fish or *belinjau*), prawn rolls, *yu tiao* with *kopi-O, bak chang, kueh lopez,* pineapple tarts…a never-ending list, because your tastebuds are so easy to please.

You may not like cooking much. But every Christmas and Chinese New Year, we used to see your early morning kitchen routine, preparing your famous *mee siam*, chicken macaroni and chicken tomato curry, as well as your signature shepherd's pie. How I miss your cooking!

My love for food, I inherited from you. My travel bug, I inherited from you. My chirpy curious nature, I inherited from you. My sense of humour, my independence, the easy way I can talk to strangers – all from you. You are my role model, Mommy.

***

It took me some time to heal myself when I went through my personal crisis. I wish you could have fully understood my pain because I really wanted to confide in you. But I knew you must have known because your memory, for some strange reason, took over and you never asked me once about my estranged husband. But you must have missed my two boys because you always asked about them.

You and Dad, 62 years of marriage. What an achievement! I have always been amazed at you and Dad, since you are so different. You used to love being out and about, while he is such a homebody. You had a social network that was always so busy that I simply could not keep up! You loved trying new things and exploring new places; he is such a creature of habit. In the end, when your illness became more serious and you were confined to home more and more, Dad has become the perfect caregiver. Your lifestyle had to change to being homebound and it suited him.

How things have turned around. You are now in perfect unison with Dad, who has been such a wonderful caregiver with his fortitude, commitment and loyalty. So blessed are you both, as I am, to watch you age gracefully in such devotional love. Even if I could not have that myself, at least I got to see it in both of you. Even if I am surrounded by more and more marital breakdowns, my relationship goal is still to grow old with my spouse. My hope in keeping it going "till death do us part" still exists, because of both of you.

***

Sometimes I fall back into wanting to be a young child again, simply because I want to have you back as my dear loving, nurturing mother, to fuss over me, clean my ears, tie my hair into ponytails…to be your little girl again. My fondest memories growing up have always been the long rides with you, whether it was taking the very first double-decker bus from Bedok Interchange to Jurong, or train rides to Johor Bahru.

Life was so much simpler then. You would take us to eat our favourite pizza and sundae. And then we would head home.

I also remember our long drives up to Frasers' Hill and Genting Highlands during the school holidays. It would be an entourage of cars that included your siblings coming along. We would spend a few days in the government bungalows because your family members were mainly teachers, like yourself, and had access to these beautiful houses. We would prepare sardine with chilli and lime and eat it up while we explored the chilly area. I do not remember much about those days, though; just sketchy memories triggered by the photos we have that I rely on and hold onto. But I know I had enjoyed my childhood very much because our extended families had frequent get-togethers. From this, you taught me how important family is.

Growing up close to your siblings, the Eurasian part of the family, has made me appreciate my Eurasian-ness more. While my mixed Peranakan and Eurasian heritage has often confused me, it has nevertheless given me a varied palate, from *babi pongteh*, Devil's curry and *sugee* cake to *apom bokwa* and *sambal belachan*. And the food was best enjoyed amidst the loud laughter of relatives at family gatherings, the humour and jokes that are so essential to life. My older cousins were always jibbing me. And since I was the youngest and one of the few girls among the boys, I learned to retaliate by sharpening my tongue and developing sarcastic comebacks.

I remember the 70s and 80s as fun times. How uncomplicated things were! You gave me a lot of freedom because I knew you trusted me. If I wanted to go to parties (functions as they were called back then), you would merely ask if Daddy was okay with it. Sometimes I lied and said yes, because it was easier to get a "yes" from you and then leave you to convince him. Looking back, I am sorry I had played you both!

I am actually quite amazed at how much you trusted me. During my first year in junior college, when my friend was visiting New Zealand with her family, you had let me go on my first holiday – without you. I was so glad you did, because I saw how fiercely independent you were and how you wanted me to be too.

So that is why I grew up to be a great solo traveller. It carried on with my job, where I had the good fortune of work trips that took me to many arts festivals overseas, tasked to find artists to perform in the Singapore Arts Festival. I have been to beautiful Tasmania, Edinburgh, London and even Avignon.

I feel so blessed because this great job that allowed me to travel was not what I had in mind growing up. I had wanted to be a teacher – just like you, your brothers and sisters. Teaching, in fact, ran in our family and even now, strangers sometimes mistake me for a teacher. It is my mannerism and tone of voice, they tell me. But I guess God had his own plan for me.

And, just like you, my love for travelling grew and I started to embark on my own retreats and pilgrimages. One thing I am so grateful for is your devotion to your faith and how I had been so much a part of your church life. I recall vividly when I was eight and attending a charismatic mass you had brought me to, but which had freaked me out. Thankfully, 35 years later, when I most needed my faith back in my life, I was prepared for it. It did not scare me so much as I knew what to expect, seeing people fall when they were touched by the Holy Spirit, with some being instantly healed of their ailments. I had my own spiritual encounter which saw me through my divorce and it made me stronger. Mommy, thank you for my spiritual formation; it was surely my faith that saw me through my most difficult times.

I never realised how much a part of your life I have been, going out with you for most of my growing up years, until your dementia had taken over you. We would sometimes bump into your church friends or former colleagues whom you had lost touch with over the years. How I could recognise so many of them amazed me. As they tried to strike up a conversation with you, I could see them getting disturbed by your response, in your lost expression and repeated questions. I had to inform them of your illness. It was sad to see some of them pulling away; it made me wonder if they did so because they were themselves afraid of dealing with this disease.

How I wish, Mommy, that your life could have gone on as normal, so that we could travel, go on mother-daughter pilgrimages together, enjoy all those foods from around the world. Mostly, I wish I could have had serious talks with you about my marriage, getting your advice about raising my boys and relying on your wisdom. Now it feels like the tides have turned and it is my turn to mother you.

Life has a funny way of turning out. We make the best of what our situation is and I have seen so much good in this. My own marriage might not have lasted but I am certainly most grateful for devoted parents who have taught me that love can truly last. I have two lovely sons whom I pray will see what committed relationships are about through the example

Jo-Anne takes her mother, Esther, around the neighbourhood, visiting some of their favourite places.

A fun photo with Mommy at Christmas.

of their grandparents' marriage. No marriage is perfect. But when I witness the steadfast love like yours and Dad's, I know that love can stand the test of time.

Thank you, Mommy, for showing me courage and positivity. For loving me so unconditionally.

Love you to the moon and back.

Your loving daughter

Jo-Anne Lee is an aspiring writer and storyteller. Her blog, *The Accidental Catholic Divorcee*, was started as part of her healing journey going through her divorce. Her greatest achievement is raising two sons, now young independent adults, while working full time, and being subservient to family needs. Now she is doing all the things she forgot she loves and has found joy again.

Mama, Live

Faith Ng

Mama,

As I write this, you are in hospital once again, for yet another infection. I try to remember when exactly you first started to decline, but I cannot quite put my finger on it. It seems like for as long as I have known you, you were always so sad, and tired, and frail. For as long as I have become conscious of you, you have always been my baby, to fiercely love and protect, as much as I am yours.

Growing up, I remember how much you hated looking at yourself. You never looked into the mirror at home. Fresh out of the shower, you would avert your gaze from the bathroom mirror and wrap yourself quickly with the towel. You would take the Prickly Heat powder and splash it all over your wet face, leaving streaks of white on your cheeks. I would laugh, watching you, and use my fingers to rub it away. Even in elevators with mirrored surfaces, you would look down at your feet, trusting me to let you know when we reached the right floor.

I have learnt to do the same. To wake up and loathe what I see in the mirror – your wide vacant eyes and heavy eye bags, my father's downturned lips, the way the ends of my hair curls disobediently, the curve of my back from too many years of bad posture. It is carved into my bones, having grown up watching and knowing it intimately – what it means to feel defective, unloved and out of place. I carry all these with me, and I wrestle with them, agonise over them, each day.

It has taken every effort in the world to remind myself, that I am deserving of love and happiness. That I am not responsible for my parents' lives, and I am not responsible for their happiness.

Mama, I wish you would know this too.

You deserve to be loved and you deserve to be happy too.

Two years ago, you fell down the stairs at home and slipped into a coma. A week before that, my water bag had broken and I was about to become a mother. You were so excited that you hailed a cab straight down to the hospital. You sat in the café for hours, waiting anxiously for updates from us. You were making frequent trips to the loo; you thought you were having a bad tummy ache, and I urged you to go home to rest. We did not know until the fall at home, that it had been a sign you were in the last stage of chronic kidney disease. Years of not wanting to take your diabetes medication and insulin injections, of ignoring doctors' appointments, of consuming soft drinks, cakes, and ice cream, had caught up with you.

Funnily enough, I had to go through the same thing as you

when I was diagnosed with gestational diabetes. I remember that the afternoon I received the call that I had GD, I went home, curled up next to Alvin on the couch and bawled into his chest. I know that it is common, that it is caused by a mechanism of pregnancy itself and it usually goes away after pregnancy, but I could not shake off the feeling that it was my fault, that I should have been more careful somehow.

I pricked my finger and took my blood sugar reading seven times a day and watched my diet. I lost 1kg and I was starving all the time. I was told that I could not lose any more weight; I had to gain it back. I brought a loaf of wholemeal bread, peanut butter and boiled eggs with me everywhere I went. I ate because I needed to, even though I was so damn sick of wholemeal bread. There were days when I pricked my fingers at least four times per reading because I was afraid of the needle, and I could not prick myself deep enough to draw blood out, or I pricked the same area too many times and odd lumps had formed under the surface of my skin. The blood sugar monitor would keep beeping and flashing ERROR 4 at me. And all I could read in that message was error, "failure", useless human being. If I could not even take a simple blood reading, how was I going to look after a baby? I started to panic. Started to fantasise about all the food that I really wanted to eat – chocolate, ice cream, white rice, *prata*, Milo, screw that, I really just wanted a sip of ice-cold lychee martini. And then I would begin to feel sorry for myself because I was so, so damn tired of having to fight off pregnancy cravings and be rigid about what I ate, and having to wrestle with the fresh wave of guilt and fear that came each time my blood sugar level shot up because I caved in and binged on something I should not have. Weak.

I understood what you were going through then, why you would say that "without sugar, life is meaningless". Sometimes, you just need something a little too sweet.

You have told me so many times the story of how, when you were a child, Coca-Cola was the most luxurious drink in the world. Your family was poor, and when they could put food on the table, they only fed the boys because boys carried on the family name. On unbearably hot and humid days, you would gaze at the glistening cold glass bottles of Coca-Cola lined up in the mama shop, and you would long to pop one open just to hear the *hissing* of gas and bubbles coming up to the surface.

When your parents forced you to stop your studies after you had completed your 'A' Levels, and you entered the working world to support the family, you made two vows to yourself – that your children would all graduate from university, and you would buy and eat and drink everything you had always wanted, starting with a bottle of Coca-Cola. It was perhaps a form of regaining control over your own life. Our family's fridge was never without the classic red cans of Coca-Cola.

One night, when I was in my last trimester, Bebe – whom you affectionately call my "little chilli padi sister" – came over to my place. She had bought me body lotion and oil. She poured the glistening oil into her hands, rubbed it onto the long red stretch marks on my belly, and in her touch I understood what she was trying to say to me: Be gentler and kinder to yourself, take care of yourself, the way I take care of you.

I thanked God for her, and because you raised her to be my best friend, I thanked God for you.

I think about what it must have been like for you as a mother – Bebe and I were twins you never expected to have, and *Jie* was the most spirited two-year-old toddler who drew on walls and put a bowl over her head in that one minute that you were not looking and cut her hair into a mess. You often talk about how Pa was overseas working for long stretches of time, and you had no support network – the in-laws disliked you and your own parents only looked after grandsons. You were on your own.

When I look at photos of you in our family albums, I see your wide vacant eyes and heavy eye bags, the way the ends of your hair curls disobediently, the curve of your back from too many years of bad posture. In your pale and skinny arms, you hold two chubby babies and a rosy-cheeked toddler. You gave yourself to us, so completely, that you almost vanished. I see a mother's boundless love, a mother's sacrifice. I know you would not want to look at those photos of yourself. But I wish you would know how beautiful and perfect you look in them; it is how you have always looked to me.

I remember you holding my baby for the first time, smelling the top of his head, kissing his cheeks. I remember how wide your smile was. I imagined your love and my love wrapping him up like a snug swaddle; our hands cradling him, supporting the back of his neck, holding up his head, hands carrying him through life.

Mama, please pull through. Please live. I am here, holding you. You have always been my baby, as much as I am yours. We will pull through. How many dark nights

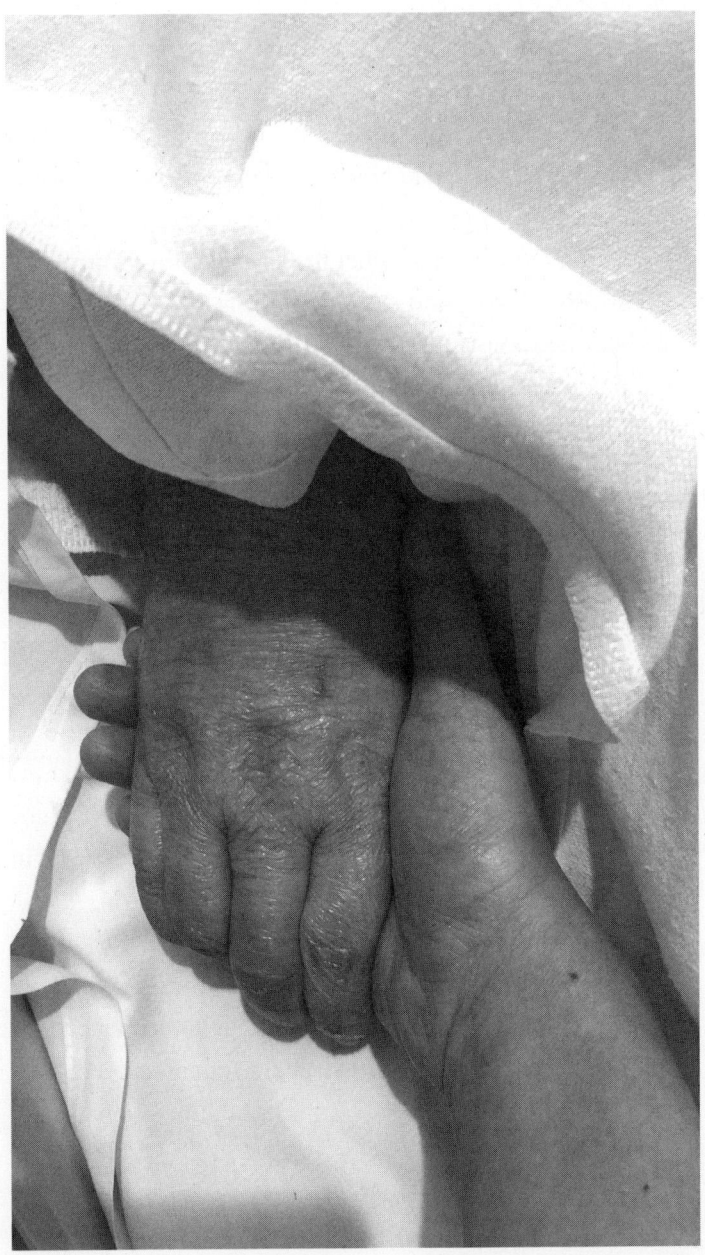

Faith holding hands with her mother and comforting her.

we have survived, nights without stars, nights with bright artificial lights in the ICU.

Just one more night. One more hour. Any minute now and the sun will rise and shine and smile widely at you once more, put a warm tender kiss on your forehead and throw you a big hug and say: "Hello, did you wait long? Silly you, I was always here, just that you could not see me. I am always here." And smile at you, smile at you, smile at you until you smile right back, my dearest mother.

Faith Ng is the Associate Artistic Director of Checkpoint Theatre. She is also a playwright and educator with a Master of Arts with Distinction in Creative Writing (Scriptwriting) from the University of East Anglia. Her plays include A *Good Death* (2018), *Normal* (2015, 2017), *For Better or for Worse* (2013) and *wo(men)* (2010). Faith was a recipient of the Singapore Creative Writing Residency in 2014. Her collection of plays, *Faith Ng: Plays Volume 1* was published in 2016 and she was conferred NAC's Young Artist Award in 2018.

Rest if You are Tired

Martha Tara Lee

Hi Mom,

It is February 12 and the first day of the Lunar New Year. It is the third reunion dinner I have had without you. When we were having the steamboat dinner Lixin had prepared, we did not speak about you, but you were in my thoughts. I thought of the banging of pots and pans when you prepared meals. I thought of how you put food on our plates and insisted we eat more. I thought of how you gave a running commentary of the cost of the food items – and inflating the prices! – as we ate and ignored you. I realise how much quieter the house has become without you – not that I miss the house being noisy. I just miss not having you around.

Dad did not give me a red packet this year. It made me recall your annual New Year and birthday red packets. Somehow, you always knew when I needed money and the size of the red packet reflected this. In turn, I want to give Dad a red packet with whatever money I have, to thank him for raising me.

My relationship with Dad is much better these days – because he is the last parent left and I cherish him more than ever. If I do not pay him attention, open my heart to him and shower him with love, then maybe one day I will regret it – just as how I have regretted I could have but did not spend more time with you.

I am sorry I was not a better daughter to you. There were many times I withheld my heart, opinions and thoughts from you. You were a different mother in your later years than the one I remember growing up with; you were once headstrong, quick-tempered, loud, smothering, and downright scary. You never talked with us but at us – through yelling or indirect conversation (talking to no one in particular while watching TV). Your voice reverberated throughout the house. I had wanted space and since I could not get it, I just withdrew into myself. After a while, distancing myself from you became a habit.

The Mom of later years was different – the Mom who had a relapse of breast cancer in 2008. You were diagnosed with stage 4 breast cancer when I was in sex school in the US, and I knew something was wrong the moment 7th Aunt asked me to take care of you.

When I came home, you thought I did not care because I was expressionless when you told me about your condition. Actually, I was shocked and numb. Being your firstborn and, like you, the headstrong one, we had exchanged cruel words in the past. When cancer struck you for the second time, I was probably not showing the love and care you had deserved because I was scared – scared of saying hurtful things to provoke you, scared to hasten your death, and scared half to death of cancer too. It was as if I was frozen emotionally and physically; I wanted to but could not have said or done more for you.

The thawing of my heart came when you were admitted for hip surgery. I saw your determination as you exercised from the hospital bed so you could regain your ability to walk quickly. I realised you did not want pity, that you were fighting for your life, for your dignity, and that you took pride in taking care of yourself. And who was I not to support you? The fear of being around you – and cancer – soon left me. I learned to appreciate the mother I had now – older, mellower and more Zen-like – rather than the one I had dreaded my whole life. We went out more, talked more, touched more, laughed more. I was proud of opening up to you. I told myself I would have no regrets if you were to pass on, since our relationship was reconciled.

The last year of your life, though, was hard for the whole family. I did not realise how hard it was until it was over – we were all just trying to keep our head above water. I was depressed, I restricted work travel and I did the bare minimum work I could get away with. I made sure I was at home in the evenings as much as possible, even when all you wanted to do was watch TV or retire to bed early. By then, you were easily tired, had a lot of dietary restrictions, less appetite, and simply did not want to go anywhere. I regretted then I did not take you out more often.

You might remember I had the most dog-sitting gigs during that period. When you asked why I kept doing this, I joked I loved doing a good deed, getting paid for it while enjoying my clients' Netflix. In reality, I needed space away from the sickness that permeated the house. Seeing you getting shockingly slimmer, smaller, and sicker was heart breaking. During those dog-sitting gigs, I noticed stress coming off, as if a lid was being taken off. It took me a while to realise what was happening. I would feel guilty about being away from you; relief from not needing to put on my game face; sadness for your suffering; waves of exhaustion that no sleep seemed to erase. And I would find myself crying in peace, away from you. The dog-sits were the much-needed respite from the endless sadness in my heart and the tears I hid from you.

The proudest moment of my life would have to being there at your deathbed – not my four degrees, not the clients I have helped. Later, my long-time friend asked me: "You have siblings. Where were they?" I had to stop myself from screaming at her: "It did not matter where they were. I wanted to be there, and I was there."

On October 16, 2018, you were admitted for water in your lungs. Even after a litre of fluid was removed, you still experienced difficulties breathing; the tumours were still producing fluid which gave you no relief. It was my birthday; I knew you must have forgotten it for the first time in my life because there was no red packet from you. As a joke, I climbed onto your hospital bed and curled up against your legs. It was at that moment Dad showed you the message from my younger sister saying it was my birthday. You were embarrassed and said you would give me a red packet when you got out. In my bravado, I said I did not care about it but I did – it was a family tradition. But all I wanted was that you came home quickly.

But with each passing day, you got progressively weaker. Initially, the hospital told us to prepare for your discharge. But such talk stopped once they realised you were too weak to get out of bed even when assisted. One night, you had an allergic reaction to a drug, foamed at the mouth, stopped breathing but were resuscitated.

Two mornings later, when you vomited blood and a piece of you came out, I ran to get the nurse. When the doctor arrived, he told you that not much could be done for you. That was when I messaged Stan (my younger brother) to return from China. You started to call everybody you knew, and many visited you that same day.

That night, you were tired, and we slept early – only to be woken up by 5th Aunt and her husband visiting. She was the last relative who came by. I knew her words affirming your strength must have brought you comfort. Later that night, Stan arrived, having just landed. You recognised him even in the dark and was so happy to see him. I knew you missed him and I was relieved you got to see him.

After he left, you spilled water on the hospital bed because you did not want to wake me and tried to reach for it yourself. When the nurses "scolded" you, for the first time in your hospital stay, you waved your hand weakly and said: "Enough. Enough. Enough." They were shocked because you had never once complained. Your "enough, enough, enough" shocked and hurt me to the core. In my frustration and helplessness, I texted Dad to scold him for forgetting to buy the baby water bottle I had told him to. Then you asked for a cold drink and drank half the apple juice I had gotten from a vending machine. You never drink cold drinks anymore – I was confused and decided not to think too much about it.

I was tired from all the commotion and could feel your eyes and love being directed at me as I fell asleep on the sofa. The next morning, a nurse informed me you had slipped into a coma and for the family to hurry to the hospital. As another nurse came in and out within the next half hour, I said to you in Mandarin: "Don't let them wake you up. Rest if you are tired."

When I saw them wheel in the resuscitation machine, I could not bear to see them revive you again. So, I headed to the shower as I needed to leave for work. When I came out, the machine was gone; nobody else was in the ward. I stood there, confused. The nurse came to me to tell me you had passed away. I was numb. I left the hospital once my siblings arrived.

Eleven days after being warded, you passed away at the Singapore General Hospital on October 27. I cried all the way to work – I had told myself countless times that I would not cry. But you had suffered so much for so long.

Within hours of me going to work and returning home, the wake was set up. Through the busyness of the day, I had no time to feel anything. That night, I could not sleep. I decided to not forget those who had helped you. I drafted my thanks to the hospital staff – as a Facebook post – before emailing it to SGH. That Facebook post was later republished on *Mothership*. I also began documenting the last week of your life. Even then I could not unwind; I could not stop crying and I could not sleep.

It was 5.22am. Something felt amiss. I meditated on it. Then it struck me: The energetic cord I had had with you was gone. I could not sleep because something was indeed missing – something more than what the human mind could comprehend. The connection I had with you was no more. It was then that the tears of grief really came. I never knew what it was like not being connected with you because I came from you – from your womb. At one point, every part of me, every cell that I am, came from you. And now without you, I am motherless. The anchor I had taken for granted all my life was gone.

For two weeks after the funeral, I did not get out of bed beyond doing the bare necessities. The funeral was so physically and emotionally exhausting that my body wanted nothing but rest. One month after you died, I was still not myself. I had to force myself to work again because there was so much left undone. I finally learned what grief was.

On Saturday September 12, 2020, I dreamed of you – the first time since you passed away (almost three years ago now).

In my dream, you were in your 30s and having some kind of white mask (like a facial mask) on. I remember stirring and freaking out in my sleep (enough to know I was asleep, and this was a dream). When I calmed down, I asked you what message you had for me. There was silence and you continued looking at me.

This was a blank stare which I was accustomed to. You used to go to our study room and stand at the door and just stare at my sister and me. I used to get irritated at this – little did I know that was your way of checking in on us, wanting to but probably did not know what to say or how to connect with us. Instead, you left us alone to focus on our studies. Space was love. What you were doing and what

Martha (right) with her mother.

you were feeling was probably incongruent – but it is what it was.

Now in this wordless stare in my dream, you were communicating more than words could say. You love me and are still checking in on me. And I love you right back... I miss you, Mom.

Sometimes, there are no words. And there is no need for words.

I am so glad for the time we had. I am proud to be your daughter: You were wilful, strong, brave and caring. And I am just like you.

Dr Martha Tara Lee is Relationship Counsellor and Clinical Sexologist as well as the founder of Eros Coaching of Eros Coaching which supports couples and individuals with their relationship and sexuality concerns since 2009. Her credentials include a doctorate in human sexuality, and Masters in Counselling. She was recognised as one of Top 50 Inspiring Women under 40 by *Her World* in July 2010, and one of Top 100 Inspiring Women by *CozyCot* in March 2011. She is the author of four books. She credits her heart for humanity and love for learning to her parents.

Letter to My Mother, Lim Siew Lian Veronica

Beverly Morata Grafton

Hey Mum,

It is coming to four years since you moved on and there has been a lot that has happened since. A big part of me is glad you left when you did; that you do not have to suffer anymore is one thing, but the fact that you do not have to suffer through all the crap that is going on in the world right now is enough for both you and me to go "Phew!" together. I can practically hear you in my head saying *"seoi neoi bao"* (bad girl) right now.

    I guess I will start at the time we had parted ways. I could not wait for you to go. Three years. Three whole years you had suffered. By the time your numbered days were on a countdown, you were in constant pain and, by no means, were you one to suffer in silence. The house was filled with your wailing, 24 hours a day. The only times you were not wailing were when you kept insisting that we bring you home. When asked where did you think your home was, you once pointed to your en suite bathroom and said: "There. That way."

Every time I heard you, every time I saw you writhing in pain (when you could move) and each time I changed your diapers, I hurt for you. I hated you for letting yourself go like that. I hated that you kept focusing on us and keeping a roof over our heads and food in our bellies instead of balancing it out with self-care.

***

You. You were the woman who had taken me to all her D&Ds because Daddy had to work (as a musician) during that time. You were the one who had introduced me to all the cool oldies I know and love, even today. You were the one who had taught me how to dance; heck, you even taught my primary schoolmates to dance as well during our ECA, Joyful Vanguard.

You took me to my first nightlife experience. Jesus, woman, you even adamantly told the management at a then-reputable nightlife establishment that you and your whole group were leaving if they did not let me through! After getting your word that I would not be allowed alcohol, they let us in. And you did all this, just so I would not feel left out that my peers were going to tea parties at the time, and you knew I loved live music and wanted to give me an education that school would never have provided.

In short, you were my hero. Daddy was my hero too, but for very different reasons. You know, many times I would think that if you and Daddy had swapped genders, it would all have made so much sense. Daddy was the one who ran the household and you did the office work. Millennials today would probably argue that you guys were so ahead of your time, but you and I both know that it was because you sucked at cooking and housework. Daddy, on the other hand, was a hands-on kind of guy. And he was a sick guitarist too. You were always so proud of him. I would never forget this nugget of advice you had told me long, long ago. You said that you always spoke highly of Daddy and that was why, regardless if he was a musician, others respected him too. You drew my attention to a few other divorced aunties and said their marriage did not work out because they had made their musician husbands feel like failures. In those days, being a musician was not considered a real job by most people but to you, it did not matter. You just cared that Daddy was nothing like the stereotype.

Back to the point I was making. Pushing you around in a wheelchair or a stroller was not how I had envisioned your old age with me. But you chose to let yourself go. You chose to put yourself last. Your favourite words were: "So what if I die? Let me die happy *lah*!" But the truth was you did not die happy. You were miserable and I hated the fact that you had the power to change it but had chosen not to.

You know, you were constantly living in fear. You even tore up the visa application to move to the US because you were afraid that you would lose *Kor Kor* and me because of the way you had disciplined us. But you had done nothing out of the ordinary, of course – just traditional Asian parent discipline with a cane and harsh words that could have crippled even Hercules. On top of that, you used to lament over our state of affairs. You would always lament why our lives had to be so difficult and why it was always one problem after another. A lot of the times, you just carried around so much hurt and negativity. I remember once when I was eight and you came into my bedroom, sat next to me gently, for the first time ever, and instead of yelling at me to wake up, you told me Daddy had lost his gig and that things were going to be tight. But before you could finish your sentence, you just crumbled in tears in front of me.

I did not know how to help you then. God knows how badly I had wanted to. But I was only eight. I did not know the first thing about giving comfort to someone. In that short time, I was forced to grow up really quickly. You, my pillar of strength, had just crumbled. What was I to say? What should I do? How do I help? Can I even help? I just sat there and stared at you. I do not remember if I hugged you or not. I guess I must have.

I have never been the most affectionate child. You always complained about that. Well into my adulthood, you complained about it too. Even when I entered motherhood, you complained to Quina about it. You always grumbled that I stopped kissing you and Daddy from the time I was nine. Well, I guess for someone who has had the capacity to feel a myriad of emotions from young, I was also quite emotionally unavailable. That must have been hell for you, huh, Mum?

You struggled to understand me, a budding artist, a Scorpio child with an aching need to feel special. I also needed my thoughts to remain mine and mine alone – something you apparently had difficulty accepting. You lived by the motto that talking about your issues will make you feel better. The thing is, my emotions are the most private part of me. You can take my body but my thoughts are not open for discussion. I was nothing like you. Maybe we might be alike in our temper – something I have outgrown over the last four years – but I am essentially nothing like you. You were an extrovert, I am not. You thrived in the company of people whilst I must have my space to recover from the energy that gets sucked out of me when I am around crowds. You found it easy to pour out your feelings to anyone who would listen.

Meanwhile, I have been with my hubby for three years and I am only now just opening up to him. What you did to me as a child is damn near unforgivable but we had managed to work that bit out, sometime when I was 34 and you were in the hospital. When I was 10, you had forced me to take out my diary during one of your scolding sessions, made me read it out loud, caned me for its contents, made me tear out pages that were thrown away because in your then-conservative mind, I was too young to have feelings like that. You basically disallowed me to feel. So, hello Repression, nice to meet you, this is my room. Get comfy because I foresee you staying in my life for a pretty long time.

During my teenage years, you would sneak into my room to read my diaries, then tell me about it when we were supposed to have those nice, cordial mother-daughter bonding talks. You would tell me that my diaries were such an enjoyable read, that it did not matter that I had written I hated you. You said I was a good writer and that I should pursue it. But I could not hear any of it, for the anger was making my blood boil, to the point it clouded my ears. All I could think of was containing my feelings and never write again, so you would never have access to my most precious thoughts.

When I told you about those episodes in the hospital, you were shocked. You did not recognise the woman that I had spoken of. I realise now that you truly had become a different woman by the time you landed in hospital. You had lost your fire, your tenacity, your drive – the very things I had loved, yet hated, about you. You allowed yourself to spiral down the rabbit hole of negativity, so much so that not only did you end up in hospital, it turned you into a regular patient there. I used to joke that you should have been given a membership card, considering the amount of time you were in and out.

It took me three years from your burial to visit your grave again. Three years to get over the hurt, hate and resentment. I could never hate anyone else because none of them ever mattered enough to me, other than you. So yes, I finally visited you last year, 2020, on your death anniversary. I had visited Dad too because, well, why not?

So many memories, Mum. Remember the time you went over to Aunty Emily's room and you let me follow? I had brought my milk bottle along. I remember walking down the hallway, then we reached her room and the next thing I remember is standing behind you on the bed where you sat, and I was hugging you from behind to rest my head on your shoulder. I remember your smell. You were chatting away and, without missing a beat, swept me up, put me on the pillow and popped my bottle in my mouth.

What about the times you had stormed into my room at 1am to tell me to shut up and go to sleep because I was waking the neighbours with my singing? And the time when I was in primary 3 and had gone to my friend's house without telling you and you had fainted?

How about all the aunties and uncles who would squeal and compliment me on how pretty or beautiful I was and you would retort: "Yes, but I am prettier." Or "I am more beautiful." You thought you were being funny but do you have any idea what that did for my self-esteem? I still have issues today.

So, yes, it has taken me three years to grieve for you.

***

Daddy left us suddenly, two years and 10 days after you. A week before my solemnisation too. Oh, how I cried then. I cried because I realised for the first time that I was well and truly on my own. I am just glad Cody got to meet Dad. Well, at least one of you got to meet him. A big part of me would like to believe that you had sent Cody my way to look after me. He is no Elvis Presley; he cannot sing, nor can he dance. But boy, he sure does try and above all, he loves me more than all the people I have dated put together.

I miss you, you know? I miss hearing your voice vibrating through your shoulders when you used to carry me to sleep. I miss the joy and pride in your face when you held your granddaughter. I miss the way you fuss over me. I miss the stupid nicknames you had given my useless exes. I miss the nicknames you had for me, like Ah-Bev, Tofu, Mei Mei, Vampire, Vainpot (in English and Cantonese) – the list goes on. I miss the times you nagged me – you even once said that one day, I will miss that. I hate to admit it but you were right.

I miss watching Bollywood movies with you while holding a box of tissues in hand. I miss going to karaoke and cringing at your singing. What I miss the most is taking you out for meals on my birthday to thank you for all the work you had done, from birthing me to bringing me up.

That line was the hardest to type through my sobbing. I have not sobbed like this in a while. I forgot that I even could.

I never got to thank you for all the things that you did teach me. You were not equipped well enough to mother me but damn, woman, how you had tried. I know I was not an easy one to parent. Ignoring all the insensitive things your stepsisters had said to you over the years about how you had brought me up, the fact is you did what none of them was capable of: You loved me. I do not believe they would know love even if it smashed them in the face with a cricket bat. What? Hehe, yes, I am still as overprotective of you as you were of me. No one can say anything bad about you – except me.

Because I am your *seoi neoi bao*.

Anyways (yes, I am not done yet), one last thing to fill you in. I leave Singapore for good this year. Thanks to the Covid-19 pandemic (glad you missed that!), I no longer have the career I used to. I am embarking on a journey to find myself anew, together with the son-in-law I wish every day that you could have met. I have lost my sense of self and everything I have known, as my reality has been swept off the table and I have to start all over again to find the real me. It is like working for years on your thesis and just when you are about to finish, your computer shorts out and fries everything. You are left with a blank page. That is where I am at now. But it just means I get to create a new

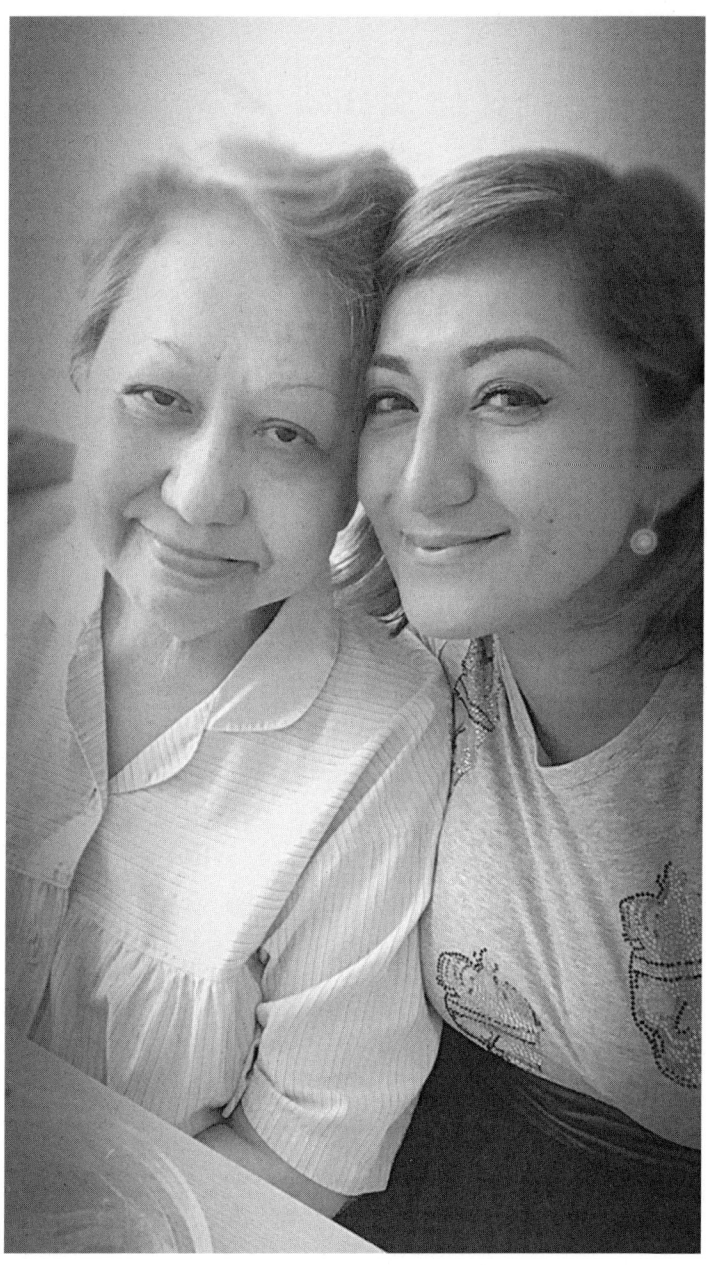

Beverley (right) wih her mother.

story. A better one than before. One I will dedicate to you and Daddy. The best one you will ever read from me. So, wherever you are now in the cosmos, do not worry about me. I am the street-smart one, remember?

I love you more than I have ever shown you.

Your loving daughter,
Bev

Beverly Morata Grafton is a daughter, a mother, a sister, a wife, a sweet stepmother, a singer/songwriter/lyricist, an anime fanatic, an aspiring writer, a budding yet talented Tarot reader, a closet comedienne, a soon-to-be homemaker, a freelance social media marketer, a cat and dog lover, a picnic-in-the-park/on-the-beach type of girl, a sad sushi roll without enough sunlight, a pretty darn great vocal coach, an emotionally aware being, ambitious, sometimes a little hard on herself, grateful to be friends with and to have worked with Felix Cheong, is ready to move on to a new chapter in her life and she hopes to have your support in her future work!

The Battle for My Left Hand

Charmaine Deng

You asked how I remember it.

I am five years old; I am sitting on my left hand so it will not get hurt.

It is 1984 – the year George Orwell imagined the world under totalitarian rule; in Singapore – which the Democratic Western world deems an autocracy – and I am a Daughter and Student, and therefore under the biggest dictatorship of all.

Sitting at the miniature desk in my yellow bedroom, it is being impressed upon me that I am a Right-Hander. You and Dad have decided that my left-handedness must be eradicated, and you are gamely executing the order.

1982, aged three: Kindergarten teacher, at wits' end, phones you because I just will not colour within the lines. You and Dad whisper behind your shut bedroom door; I know it is about me.

1984, aged five: You have tried to frustrate the southpaw out of me. You have made me sit on my left hand. The mugs of crayons, snacks and drinks are on my distant right.

But, table arrangements are not enough to stop nature – or at least, not mine. My left hand persists, reaching stubbornly for Crayolas and crackers, even if it means having to stand up.

This is a decade pre-Internet; there are no forums yet where mothers exchange clever ways to break their children's spirits. Out of ideas and patience, you lie in wait, and sting the back of my "wrong" hand with a thin bamboo cane every time I lift it.

Left is the opposite of right, I am learning, but so is wrong, and I am both.

2004, aged 25: The word "sinister" comes from the Latin for "left". The Bible tells us, after God separates the good from the bad, He puts the sheep on his right and the goats on his left.

I ask why you had felt so strongly that I must not be left-handed, and you shrug. Twenty years later, it is a minor issue. Without looking up from your phone, you say simply: "The world is made for right-handers."

Of course, you are right. The majority, is right. From fridge doors to fountain pens, scissors to spiral-bound notebooks, the world is easier for those who fit its norms.

According to the Bible, goats are bad. According to the Chinese Zodiac, I am a goat.

1984, aged five: I am dragging my feet behind you, on the long walk from our block to the next. My slippers are on wrong, because you would not help me with them. Mothers do not help their children with footwear when they have had it up to here and are giving them away.

The old lady in the next block lives alone and has no children, you said. She could use a naughty girl like me as a servant. We had seen her shuffling around, eyes down, in the supermarket. She smelt of mothballs. It is her you fear becoming now, isn't it? Becoming alone. A death before dying.

I try to match my stony face to yours, ignoring neighbours hungry for drama. Neither of us want to give in, to admit we need the other. I am carrying my pillow; a plastic bag you thrust at me bumps against my leg. I sneak a peek in the bag: Just two pairs of panties, which you had packed for me. Somehow this, of everything that has been happening, breaks me. I am sorry, I cry. I will be good. I will do whatever you want. Please don't give me away.

1984, aged five: I just want to scribble, and if I cannot do it with one hand, I will just do it with the other. So I teach my right hand to write. I make sure to use it to turn pages when you read to me. We are halfway through *The Little Mermaid*. You pause to coo: "See, if a mermaid princess gave up her tail and her sweet voice for some legs, you can use your right hand, right?" Persuasion and punishment; carrot and stick.

Fine, I concede – but only when someone is watching. Alone, I stubbornly hold books in my left, and read about the dumb little mermaid's choice backfiring–the prince loves another woman, as they do, and she will become sea-foam. I brush my hair with my left hand before bed, looking hard in the mirror.

1987, aged eight: The cane has become an extension of your right hand. It delivers correction whenever I go off-book – such as now, when I come home with 99 per cent on a test.

I hold my left palm out to face your sentence. Since it is the hand less used, it can afford to be sore.

It is not the marks I am being punished for, you clarify: It is because I was careless. You do not demand perfection.

1993, aged 14: Even though you do not demand perfection, I am in a prestigious programme in a prestigious all-girls school, my path to an illustrious government career all mapped out for me.

I am not unhappy. Not yet. With your encouragement, I have not stopped penning *précieux* poems and prose – it is a respectable hobby among scholarly teens. You read everything I show you, even stick some of it up on the fridge. I even write a play then-Prime Minister Lee Kuan Yew actually comes to see – surprisingly small for a giant, but a presence so immense we know the moment he enters the Jubilee Hall theatre at Raffles Hotel, even before whispers reach us backstage, even though the houselights are completely dark.

But when I step onstage, it is your face I look for first.

After the performance, the Father of Singapore shakes my right hand cursorily. I curb the urge to curtsey, then turn to see if you are proud.

I continue drafting amateur novels and filling in aptitude tests with the same hand, and there is no struggle. Like Margaret Atwood's rat, I am free to go anywhere – as long as I stay inside the maze.

1994, aged 15: I am the same age now as the little mermaid was when she rose to the surface of the ocean and everything changed.

I play Nirvana on repeat. The vicarious angst of their violent guitar riffs is just enough to keep me from acting on my own teen spirit. Also, I have a small crush on their beautiful, tormented frontman, Kurt Cobain, who plays guitar left-handed. He was also forced by his father to switch from left to right as a child.

Cobain shoots himself in the head. He is found dead with the shotgun barrel in his left hand.

I resolve to wear black for a month, but only manage one morbid week before you kidnap the Nirvana t-shirt I have been wearing over my school uniform. It needs washing, you say. I never see it again.

1994, aged 15: I am in bed; I have just fallen asleep, at the end of a packed school day, which I will wake in a few hours to repeat. You burst into my room, cane in hand, light streaming behind you through my flung-open bedroom door like a halo of righteous anger.

Cornered in my bed, I make out that I had not placed the dinner dishes in the "right" order after washing them. The sound, the fury, signifies everything wrong with me.

1994, aged 15: I am in bed; I have just fallen asleep, at the end of a packed school day, which I will wake in a few hours to repeat. We have fought over something nobody remembers anymore. You open my door gently, but I have learned to listen for the way it creaks. Eyes closed, I feel you standing over me. I stiffen. What did I forget to do now?

You sigh heavily. My mattress sinks under your weight. Your hand smooths my hair away from my forehead. Your fingers are rough and garlic-scented from cooking lunch and dinner, countless lunches and dinners. Tears gather behind my lids.

It is your left hand. Your left holds the garlic, your right holds the knife.

1995, aged 16: My little sister comes quietly into my room after I have stormed away from another row with you, white and wordless.

"Why do you have to fight with Mum so much?" she asks. "Can't you just be more obedient?"

1996, aged 17: The time you said our family would be perfect, if not for me.

1996, aged 17: There is a moment for a teenage girl when she does not belong to anyone. I am between self-absorbed boyfriends, and a devastating disappointment to you – too old for the cane, but apparently too young for boys. You resort to scathing words and withhold phone, party and pecuniary privileges to keep me in line. Dispossessed, I am exhausted with potent, impotent adolescent wrath.

Being a Girl has been simple in a top all-girls' school where there was nothing we could not do. It is being a Woman which will take learning – but that cannot now be from you.

1997, aged 18: The pre-college watershed. I am strung helplessly between all the futures I want to live. Thorny, sulky, estranged from you, I rely instead on books, music and serendipity, for guidance.

A boy buys me a Radiohead poster with my favourite lyrics on it: "An empowered and informed member of society, pragmatism, not idealism … Calm, fitter, healthier and more productive. A pig in a cage on antibiotics." When I wake in the mornings, I bask in its irony like sunlight. It sums up everything I fear government-career me will become, in one easy-to-shudder-at package. Of all the lives I want, this is not one.

Someone gives me my first copy of Rilke's *Letters to a Young Poet*. I read that famous passage aspiring writers through the ages agonise over, and it creates no conflict in me: "Go into yourself. Search for the reason that bids you write; find out whether it is spreading out its roots in the deepest places of your heart, acknowledge to yourself whether you would have to die if it were denied you to write."

Check, Herr Rilke. "Then build your life according to this necessity," he intones, in a voice like God's – like Morgan Freeman's, but with a German accent.

1998, aged 19: And so, where everybody else turns right, I turn left. I need to find my way, and I will do it alone if I have to.

My peers head off to the most esteemed universities in the world; I stay behind. Scholarships are the opposite of freedom, and I lost your support some time ago, so I will work through college. I eschew Law for Literature – a first, I am told, by a huffy Law faculty member sent to talk me off the ledge.

I quote E.E. Cummings grandly at him: "To be nobody-but-yourself – in a world which is doing its best, night and day, to make you everybody else – is to fight the hardest battle which any human being can fight." He is not impressed.

2003, aged 24: I marry poster-boy much too young; the ring sits uncomfortably on my left hand. I will divorce him three years later, partly because I married him to get out of your house, and partly because it turns out he does not get irony.

I am busy carving out a career as a journalist. Even if it is not the sort of writing I wanted to do, I get to play with words for a living – and that is all that matters.

2006, aged 27: I am promoted at work. Every month, you cut out my "Letter from the Editor", and carefully add the clipping to a colourful album.

I now write almost exclusively on a keyboard. Meaning, with both hands.

2013, aged 34: You have grown old while I was not looking. I have been a head taller than you for years, but your hands — which had once held mine as I learned to walk, learned to write, learned to roller-skate — are bony now, green veins show through translucent skin.

Are these really the same hands that hurt me every time you were angry? They are so small.

2017, aged 38: *The Women's History of the World* suggests humans evolved to be predominantly right-handed because of mothers. Women have carried babies on the left side of their bodies since the dawn of time, making it necessary to complete all sorts of tasks with their right hand alone.

Why on the left? Because nothing comforts a child like its mother's heartbeat. Yours. Mine. Even through difficult years, even through enormous differences, enormous distances.

1972: You are 19 years old. You are making your way from the kampong so small it did not even have its own police station, 600km south via Kuala Lumpur, to the electric lights of Singapore.

You need to find your way, and you will do it alone if you have to.

Away from the draughty wooden house you had never left for a night, the zinc roofs, the kerosene lamps, the school with the benches and the earth floor. Your sprawling family. The mother who stripped you naked and whipped you in the yard, who will never stop asking when you are coming to visit again. Your heart will forever be in two places at once.

But you will travel the world, every continent of it. You will love and be loved. You will find meaning, and understanding. You will make mistakes, and there will be time to fix them.

Do you see it? Where everybody else had turned right, we had turned left. The stubbornness you hated in me, my will you had tried so hard to break – is yours.

2019, aged 40: "No need to hurry. No need to sparkle. No need to be anybody but oneself," says Virginia Woolf. I have high tea with high-ranking, prematurely-grey diplomat friends, and meet you and Dad for dinner once a month. In both cases, we avoid difficult topics, and laugh instead about how I always get lost because I still mix up my right and left.

My right arm has "writer" tattooed on it. I have a gratifying collection of fountain pens, which I can use without smudging.

My left hand is free of cumbersome jewellery. I use it to stir strong coffee, hold cigarettes, cup lovers' faces when we kiss.

I am 40 years old. My left hand is free.

Charmaine Deng is a former lifestyle journalist and editor. She is interested in memory and identity-construction, and is working on her first novel.

A Necessary Detour

Nanny Eliana

Your face was one of the many faces I remembered only because I had seen it often. It was a familiar blur among many familiar blurs at weddings, funerals and my neighbourhood's super sundry store on Sunday mornings. I knew you only by your first name. I knew you had two daughters and a husband, but no other clue that might have been telling of our connection, by blood or law.

That day, after I had defied a 7pm curfew for the 6th time in a month, my adoptive father stormed into my room howling, fighting back tears.

He pushed my books off the bookshelves, threw my clothes out of the cupboards, and turned my bed onto its side.

I stood there watching him, refusing to speak or cry.

Then these words shot out of his mouth: "You are not my child!"

When my adoptive mother came home and discovered I knew the truth, she cried for three days. Her face remained red and swollen afterwards, yet she carried on cleaning, cooking and marking her students' assignments.

I was not yet 19.

My adoptive father knew revealing the truth would not inspire me to comply. So, he did what he did best, which was to eject me out of his household with the force of disowning an apostate, whore or addict, despite me being none of these things.

He returned me to you, like you would return a broken kettle to a store.

I thought I was merely returning to ordinariness. An ordinariness which seemed to have blessed every single person I knew outside of that immediate family but me.

I wondered what it would be like to wake up every day without having to read the temperature of the household with the hair on my forearms, calculating if what I had planned for the day would invite any wrath, and if it did, whether I would have the stomach for it.

I wondered what it would be like to live where conversations were neither interrogations nor crippled by fear of physical pain or abandonment. And where publicly accepted facts dropped at the dinner table were not met with howling and thumping, no matter how excited the conversation. (Years later, upon establishing that I had, in fact, not run away from home but was abandoned by my adoptive father, his younger siblings confirmed that howling and thumping were hallmarks of his behaviour from before he enrolled at the Police Academy.)

I wondered what it would be like to shrug off the yoke of my adoptive father's expectations that I become a hijab-wearing criminal lawyer. And be the youngest child – your youngest child – a position I was born into but never had the opportunity to assume.

In my mind, the youngest child was allowed to climb a tree, fail a test, or two, or three at school, sleep over at a friend's place over the weekend, feed and pet puppies and kittens on the street – all with no long-lasting repercussions.

Over the numerous Hari Raya visits to your home, I saw that you had been used to working hard and living simply. Your dedication in raising your two daughters – my elder sisters – who were now working adults, had begun to pay off.

On most visits, on the living room table, there was a small posy of flowers – usually chrysanthemums from the wet market – and store-bought *kueh* alongside those that you had made with the new Kenwood oven my sisters had bought for you. The shrill chorus of "Kuch Kuch Hota Hai", the theme song of a Hindi movie of the same name, repeated in the background.

"*Dah tengok banyak kali, tapi tiap kali tengok masih ketawa, masih nangis,*" you said. *I have watched the movie many times but I still laugh and cry each time.*

On one visit, Eldest Sister came home, having bought you *mee goreng mamak* from the hawker centre where the family usually bought their takeaways. Wearing day-old uniform that had been greased and smoked by frying patties over a griddle, she force-smiled at everyone in the room. She changed into shorts and an oversized T-shirt and disappeared into the kitchen. I never saw her again until after you and I were properly introduced to the family as biological mother and daughter.

I wanted to be loved, like how close-knit families with very little love each other, even those who did not seem to have any love to give.

"*Bapak ko tak sihat,*" you said. *Your father is not well.*

You said this to me the day I came to you with two suitcases containing everything I owned. And to every other visitor who had felt the unsettling weight of *Bapak* staring at the space above their heads, but were too polite to ask what was wrong.

You would ask *Bapak* a series of questions meant for the visitors to hear.

"*Dah makan, kan?*" *You have eaten, haven't you?*

"*Dah mandi kan?*" *You have taken a shower, haven't you?*

"*Dah pergi rumah mak, kan?*" *You have been to Mother's house, haven't you?*

"*Dah,*" he would say.

My hope for ordinariness and love of a close-knit family evaporated not long after we waved my adoptive parents goodbye for good. Hearse-like, their seven-seater Honda rolled out of the carpark, and picked up speed when it came onto the main road.

Bapak had been gainfully employed at a coffeeshop nearby for the past few years. He did not have much time between scraping leftovers from plates into wet bins and wiping tables with a damp rag to stare at the space above people's heads. But within weeks of my return, he had displayed "upsetting behaviour" at work and it was decided that he stay at home.

I had learned to lock myself in the bedroom whenever I was home alone. *Bapak* was mostly in either of two states – incapacitated by lithium or about to lunge at me with his fist, or whatever was within reach.

He was the constant shadow at home. In fact, shadows seemed to coalesce with his own. Hard-bellied and diabetic, he had short arms and fingers that were often scaly with eczema. His fingers were barnacled with stones he claimed held magical powers. His clothes hung on him like wet rags, even when they had been freshly laundered. On some days, he stunk of muddy salt, and had to be cajoled to shower.

One afternoon, he showed me his collection of stones. He rattled them in an old Quality Street Sweets tin as he retrieved them from the top of the refrigerator. From it, he retrieved a ring with a large green stone the shape and size of a quail's egg. He held it up to the light, as if to see through it, and slipped it onto a stubby finger.

"*Ini dari laut,*" he said. *This is from the sea.*

That night I pondered the truth of that, when the smell of *kemenyan* (incense) had filled each room, the intermittent waft of swampy sea just perceptible beneath it. *Bapak* was sitting in his chair in the living room. He was shaking his legs as if the ground beneath him was quaking, and muttering under his breath what sounded like verses from the *Qur'an*, but were probably not. The skin on his forearms and legs was flaking like castor sugar falling on a cake.

He leapt up and pulled a punch as I entered the kitchen for a glass of water. But as suddenly as he had leapt up, he dropped his shoulders, turned slack-jawed, and wandered into the living room. I saw the glint of the house keys in his hand before he opened and shut the main door behind him.

That night I could not sleep. Once or twice, something or someone cast a shadow over the bedroom window facing the corridor, as if looking in.

When I finally drifted to sleep, Eldest Sister entered the room at what must have been six in the morning. She popped on the lights. In preparation for her work day, she rummaged through and retrieved her things, making the noises one would make when putting her family's needs before her own.

Rain had begun to fall in thick, loud sheets. I could barely hear the jingling of keys and creaking open of the main gate to allow *Bapak* in and Eldest Sister out.

I cringed, recognising the timbre of Eldest Sister's voice in my own.

She asked: "*Bapak pergi mana malam tadi?*" Where did you go last night?

"*Pergi kedai.*" To the shop.

"*Mana ada kedai bukak malam-malam buta!*" There are no shops open that late at night!

But *Bapak* was home and safe, and she had to leave for work. So, nothing else was said.

Between the first incident and your death, *Bapak* had attacked or attempted to attack me five times. The second incident was hard to miss. He had punched me under my left eye hard enough that the stones had fallen off his rings, and the skin under my eye had torn. Somehow, I had managed to wrest him off, run to the bedroom and lock myself in until you returned.

The next day, you and Middle Sister sat him up in his chair and scolded him.

"*Bapak pukul Nan ni dah kenapa?*" Why did you hit Nan?

"*Ada firasat!*" I had a premonition!

"*Tak habis-habis firasat! Kan kita dah cakap! Jangan pukul orang!*" You and your premonitions! We have told you not to hit people!

"*Dia nak bunuh aku! Buang dalam sungai!*" *She wants to murder me! Throw me into the river!*

Between the first incident and your death, he disappeared for hours on end on some days. One day, after an unusually long excursion, he came home, having had several of his upper teeth extracted.

I reported to you and Middle Sister that he had come stabbing the bedroom door with a kitchen knife while I was in the room and home alone. You found that he had been hiding, if not flushing his precious lithium down the toilet when he should have taken them.

You and Middle Sister would then sit him up in bed or in his chair in the living room, scold him, threaten to call the men in white from Woodbridge to take him away. *Bapak* did not like the men in white from Woodbridge, and he promised to calm down.

I wandered into the kitchen one day. I could not remember when or why I was there. You were sitting at the dining table, wringing your hands. Your eyes were clouded over by a not-too-distant past.

"*Dulu pernah Bapak tidur dengan parang bawah bantal. Satu kali hampir dia tikam aku malam-malam buta. Kalau aku tak jerit kuat-kuat, aku dah mati dah.*" *Once, your father used to sleep with a parang under his pillow. One night, he attempted to stab me with it in the middle of the night. If I had not screamed, I would have been dead.*

I did not report further incidents to you.

I had begun to spend much of my time outside, coming home only to sleep when everyone else was home. I had begun to discover things I enjoyed doing with people and at places I liked, and you wanted to know and understand, but would probably not.

You had been told the factory where you assembled circuit boards for money no longer required your services.

So, you were home all day, every day. The rare instance I was home in the day, you would be shouting at Hindi movies as they played on TV.

"*Apasal muka dia putih tapi leher hitam?*" Why is her face so white but her neck so black?

"*Perut macam tu pun boleh masuk TV?*" She can come on TV with a stomach like that?

"*Yang in takde pinggang, takde punggung!*" This one has no waist, no bum!

"*Hidung pesek macam tu pun boleh masuk TV?*" She can come on TV with a flat nose like that?

"*Muka dia manis, tapi sayang hidung pesek!*" She has a sweet face, but such a pity her nose is flat!

That last statement sounded like it was thrown at me, demanding my response.

I turned around to look at you: Your dark brown skin, broad nose, the cowls of loose dark skin under your sunken eyes, the spare wisps of eyebrows above them, your fine matt of curly hair showing the first sprays of white. Your nasolabial lines were so deep that the skin around your mouth seemed to stretch taut around your thin lips. You were obviously scowling but because your front teeth were uneven, your mouth often seemed to be involuntarily open. Depending on which angle I looked at you, it could be interpreted either as a smile or smirk.

And with your eyes still on the TV, you shrieked: "*Ko jangan tengok aku takde mata eh! Kalau bukan pasal aku, ko pun tak cantik macam ni lah!"* You do not look down on me, okay! If not for me, you would not be this pretty!

I found *Bapak* sitting on the toilet bowl, fully clothed. When he saw me, he stood up, like he had been weighed down by sandbags, and wandered out, the hems of his trousers smearing moisture across the kitchen floor.

Eldest and Middle Sister probably thought your retrenchment was an opportune time for you to rest. You had begun working since your mid-teens, picking up after residents of black and white bungalows, long before labour laws for minors were enacted or at least, consistently enforced.

I thought your retrenchment must have triggered a series of mostly unexplainable mishaps: Symptoms of your body giving way to life's burdens which had swollen and festered over time, squeezing from you your every last breath, and snuffing every little light within you.

At first, you could not walk, but the doctors said you did not have a stroke or a heart attack, and it did not seem like a neurological disorder, and so to prevent osteoporosis and muscular atrophy from setting in, you were prescribed daily physiotherapy sessions.

Then you could not see, and it was not a diagnosable blindness either. On some days, a shadow hovered over your right eye and you could only make out shadows and shapes; on some days, the same shadow hovered over the left. On some days, you could make out colours and faces through the shadows; on some days, you could not. Tests did not show up any known disease for which there were available therapies.

In the meantime, the sisters stocked up on thick socks, blankets, Vicks, walking frames, fresh fruit, heat rubs, foam pillows, vitamin supplements and Hindi movie VCDs.

What little I had done for you in the time you were hospitalised – which was increasing in length and frequency – was merely incidental. Middle Sister had taken to applying aloe vera gel on your eyelids with her fingers to lighten them. Sometimes, I took over. I brought you flowers on some days when I visited, massaged your feet when you asked, entertained your sisters and aunts' anxious chatter when they visited. A glimmer fending off a looming and certain darkness.

Soon after, you died while in a coma, after you had been taken off the ventilator which had mechanically inflated your lungs for several days. You had just turned 50.

Your passing freed me from the only bond that had kept me in a home where I was never wanted, and should not have re-entered.

I could not say I love you; certainly not the kind of love that could have sprung between us had you raised me through hardship, the way you had raised my elder sisters.

I could not say I wish I had known you more, although there had been certainly more of you that had been eaten away by *Bapak*'s illness.

Yet, upon your passing, I felt relief in ways you would never have known.

And perhaps, this was your true legacy.

Nanny Eliana first published her writing as a teenager, in local Malay daily *Berita Harian,* and in the now-defunct *Teens* magazine. In 2005, the year her birth mother died, she established Bridges M&C, a communications agency, out of a shophouse cubbyhole. Now a 10-man team, Bridges M&C has a registered office in Kuala Lumpur and with regional partners, serves the medical and healthcare industry in the Asia-Pacific. A recipient of the National Arts Council Arts Creation Grant in 2010, Nan's single focus had been on establishing and building her business until the Covid-19 pandemic, when she rediscovered her love for creative writing and water colour painting.

My Mother and Her Unprintable Life

Christine Chia

So much of your life was unprintable in English, a tongue you could never wrap your tongue around, despite speaking Hokkien, Teochew, Japanese and Thai. You spoke Thai best, while I struggled with four stock Thai phrases to field calls from your friends: "She is out having fun/She is bathing/She is not in/Telephone."

The phone was how I knew you were in the hospital, because we had stopped talking to each other for a year. We had stopped talking because your last lie to me was just too preposterous. My last words to you, not knowing they were such, were, in Hokkien: "This lie is just too big."

The phone was ideal. Ideal because distant. Distance was necessary because you were still quick to hit anyone who crossed you, especially if they were your own. I wonder if there are phones in heaven?

Who would you call? Maybe your best friend, Auntie Nita. She still dreamed about you for months after your funeral. I would call her to find out the latest in the astral realm because you almost never appeared in my dreams. Once, she dreamed that all of you – the gang of four Thai aunties – were at a buffet, eating Japanese food. You were always hankering for sushi, and often brought K, your firstborn grandson, to eat it.

Maybe you might call your "Caltex son", the flamboyantly fey Indian petrol attendant whom you used to talk long into the night with, complaining about Brother's marital woes. In the condolence book, he had signed himself off as your "Caltex son". He really loved you, and likely more than us. Once he saw the funeral tentage being set up across the road from the petrol station, he walked over and started telling us what a generous mother you were, always giving food to all the Caltex petrol attendants. His large eyes welled up as he was talking about you, and the tears rolled down but he made no attempt to wipe them off. Brother and I stood there, numb and tired. I found it hard to look at him and his uncomplicated grief, so I looked at the tree, the overhead bridge, the sandy soil, and then finally back at him. Brother was smoking. I know you hoped he had kicked the habit but it was not to be. We were never going to cry for you like he did.

We could not cry because we were too tired. Because we remembered too much of the bad times. Like the time you took a bamboo pole and beat up Brother's old girlfriend because she would not break up with him. Like the time you took a fallen tree branch lying on the ground outside Katong Shopping Centre and threw it after him like a javelin when you caught him playing truant there and he ran away from you like the Furies were upon him. Like the time you shoved his wife (not the girlfriend – she finally got the message after the beating) while she was pregnant because she was simply there when you were exploding. She should have removed herself, you had said.

I removed myself from you when I was 18. It was a move years in the making. If I were ever asked what I wanted to be when I grew up, I would have said: "Something. Anything. Just not here." I was looking at rental advertisements in *The Straits Times* classifieds when I was 13, and had started working part-time when I was 14 to save up for it because I could read the signs that I needed to leave. You told me I needed to leave when you knocked down the wall of my room to make the living room bigger so that you could have more space to entertain your friends/run a home business. You told me I needed to leave when you made me share a room with Brother but never got round to getting another bed, so I had to sleep on the floor. Last, you told me studying was useless for a girl and that I would be better off doing some real work, so that I had to study for my exams standing up in the squatting toilet of the home so that I would not set you off. The other toilet of the house was just next to my toilet-cum-study corner, so I could tell which of your friends had drunk too much beer from the velocity of their piss.

Maybe you might call me. But would I pick up your call? What could you say to me that I would understand, deafened as I was by the thunder of your curses, blinded by the lightning of your fists?

"If I knew you were going to be like this, I would have squeezed you back up my birth canal and choked you to death."

To such sound and fury, my only recourse was silence. And hard work. Hard work that paid off when the National University of Singapore gave me the scholarship that freed me from you. Even though I never heard from you in the four years I was there, I was still on the lookout for you. I avoided meeting friends in the Katong/East Coast area because I did not want to bump into you. I would look up any new buses I had to take in case they passed by one of your haunts. Entire parts of the city were off-limits to me, radioactive because you might be there.

Some of these radioactive areas include:

The Immigration Checkpoint Authority (ICA) Building in Lavender, where you calculatedly had a full-on fit when it was clear that your two-week social visit pass would not be renewed. Blessedly, you had coolly told me that you were going to throw just such a fit in front of the approving officer before we walked in, because we had applied for the social visit pass too often. I was confident that the rule of law in Singapore would be impervious to such theatrics and had told you so, and to not embarrass yourself (or me) with such *wayang*. But I was wrong. Spectacularly wrong. You threw yourself into the crying fit with such gusto that nobody else could have thought it was an act. You were kneeling, crying, striking your head on the floor and everyone else could only look at you. You caused such a commotion that the officer approved the social visit pass just to get you off the floor and let normal business proceed. This tall and well-built Indian lady ICA officer, in her starchy navy-blue uniform, was no match for you;

Geylang, where we used to help Auntie Nita deliver her Thai food to some of the brothels. In one of your rare moments of calmness, as we were walking to Aljunied MRT station, you told me that you knew you could never be a prostitute, even if the money was "much easier", because "I am just too bad-tempered";

Golden Mile, of course, both the Complex and the Tower, because you were a well-known figure in both places and I bore more than a passing resemblance to you;

East Coast Road, and Siglap, because they were where you and Auntie Nita stayed. At your funeral, I learned that just the night before your heart attack, you were still cycling around the neighbourhood, and thinking about cycling over to Auntie Nita's place to give her some cough medicine. How could you be gone when you had so much vigour in you? She could not believe it and neither could I. I only believed it when I saw your cremated bones in front of me and even then, even after seeing the white, brittle curve of what was your pelvis before it was placed in the urn, I still struggled to believe it.

Now that you are no longer here, and no longer in Auntie Nita's dreams, I wonder where you are. I hope you are happy, finally, because you were never happy for as long as I knew you, or from what little I knew of you. When I called Auntie to ask if there was a new dream this year, she said, "No – I think she finish all her business here already. Good for her *lah*, not to be in my dream anymore."

Did you finish all your business here, Mother? I wonder if I had ever wronged you in a previous life? I suspect I could have, because it would partially explain what happened. One funny story Auntie Nita told me was quite telling. She said she once started an argument with you by stating: "Your side of the family is full of bad-tempered hotheads." Of course, you took the bait.

There is not much I can find out about your side of the family, other than this titbit. You were not in the habit of dishing the dirt on your siblings. I wonder if you can read both my books now, or even the unpublished play that was completed shortly before you passed, or even see the short film, *Let Me Kill My Mother First*, where Yeo Yann Yann played you to furious perfection, her rage simmering or boiling over in every frame.

One thing I learned from my years with you was to never sit still. If you sat around, you were asking to be a target. To this day, I still feel better walking or doing housework than sitting around.

There is probably not enough therapy in the world for all the wounded daughters out there. Or all the wounded mothers. I wonder if I ever mattered enough to you to hurt you. Maybe not. I was not important enough to you for you to worry about me. I know this because your "Caltex son" told me so.

"Did my mother ever talk about me to you?"

"Err. A bit. Mostly about your brother. She worry about him."

"She did not worry about me?"

"No, she did not worry about you. She said: 'I do not worry…because she is like me.'"

Am I really like you, Mother? I tried so hard not to be like you. I tried so hard not to be a narcissist. I tried so hard not to hate myself. Because much as you hated me, you hated yourself more. No matter how much you beat me and Brother up, you beat yourself more by working topsy-turvy hours. In the year before you died, people said you often worked through the night making Thai desserts till 5am, and then slept till 11am. You were punishing yourself with shift work when you did not have to. Shift work has been proven to be a major health risk but I am not sure you knew that. Or cared. Because you always liked to push your luck, even when you were not a very lucky person.

The first piece of bad luck you had was to remarry a man as bad-tempered as yourself. Your second husband (not my father) gave as good as he got, and perhaps even more. The second piece of bad luck you had was to have a daughter like me, unforgetful, unforgiving: I blocked your number, finally, after you pushed it too far. You had asked me to take you on a holiday with Auntie Nita because the other aunties had children who took their mothers on holidays, but where was I?

I was fine with paying your bills, insurance and other expenses, but going on a holiday? With you?

"Why you never take me go holiday? I not your mother?"

"I can give you the money and you can go on a holiday with Auntie Nita and her daughter. But I cannot go."

"Cannot? Why?"

"Don't you remember what you did to me?"

"What I do you?"

"You do not remember beating me?"

"So long ago. Cannot forget?"

"I cannot forget it."

"*Aiyoh*, I beat you once. Why you cannot forget?"

I lost it. Once. This was gaslighting on steroids.

"You did not beat me once. You beat me almost every day, even when I worked for you like a dog."

"Once. Only once."

Christine celebrates her birthday with her mother and brother.

"This lie is just too big!"

And that, laughably, was why I blocked you. It was a silly thing for you to lie about, because you had beaten me up in front of so many different people, in public, for years. It was also traumatising for other people to see you beating me, did you know? When someone is shopping at Bugis Junction or Parkway Parade, they just want to shop, not face a moral dilemma about whether to intervene in domestic violence. And they never did, of course. All kids are brats. All children are asking for it. It is not my business. She might beat me up too. Just walk away.

Christine Chia is the author of *The Law of Second Marriages* (Math Paper Press) and a sequel, *Separation: A History* (Ethos Books). She also co-edited the groundbreaking anthology *A Luxury We Cannot Afford* (Math Paper Press,

2014) and a sequel, *A Luxury We Must Afford* (2016). In 2017, she co-edited *Lines Spark Code* (Ethos Books). Her work has appeared in the *Washington Square Review*, *Brooklyn Poets Anthology*, *Unfree Verse*, and the W!ld Rice play, *Another Country*. Her first play was read at Centre 42's First Acts. She is working on a second play and a third book of poetry.

Letter to My Mother[*]

Tania De Rozario

I want to start with a cliché. To ask how long it has been. To scan the apartment, comment on what has not changed, ask questions about what has. To muse about how time flies, how death has a way of smoothing over the rough edges of life, the sharp pointed corners of broken relationships.

But I can't. Because I know exactly how long it has been. The last time I was here, it was 2003. You were in your bedroom, working. Gramps was taking a nap. Nana was in the living room, watching television. This is the amber memory of my last day here, frozen for a decade and a half. I left, and three of you were here. Today, everyone is gone. I return the same way I left – alone.

Do you remember my leaving? Did you see through all my stealth? I could not afford to move out all at once, so I packed whatever would fit into three plastic bags each day, and transferred all of it to my new place after work. Three was the magical number. Small enough not to warrant suspicion,

---

[*] "Letter to My Mother" was originally published in *Journal – Centre for Stories* in 2020.

substantial enough for someone who did not own much. By the end of the week, I had moved everything I needed. The next day, I just did not come home.

Did you ever wonder where I had gone?

I have so many questions about your apartment. About the objects it houses. As with most people who have lived in one place for many years, life does not change as much as accumulate. Closets brimming with clothes – all yours. Leftover medication from the cancer. Electronics thick with rust, carpets fat with the corpses of dead unidentifiable bugs, books jacketed with years of dust, pamphlets concerning single parenthood and "how to bring your child back to Christ".

Fifteen years we lost to each other. Perhaps in another life, we are making up. Perhaps in another life, I had no reason to leave. Perhaps in that other life, I know the names of all these strangers pressed between the pages of the 25 photo albums I am lugging home. Perhaps I knew my father.

I must admit, as I pillage your belongings, I think about how they might become useful to me. Maybe I will make drawings from these photographs. Maybe these documents can be turned into found poems. Maybe all these personal belongings will become an installation piece about "Archiving Family". Archives are very popular these days with artists, you know. Very hip. Very now.

If I sound cold, it is because I am. The minute I understood my trauma had currency, you stopped being my mother and started being material. This icy attitude is how I survived. The day you got your church friends to exorcise the "lesbian demons" from my 12-year-old body, you broke my heart in the process, so do not blame me for its malfunctioning, for this wintery ability to milk you for all you are worth. Make no mistake – you made me this way.

Packing up your apartment has really been the mildest part of this logistical nightmare. Thanks to your death, I have also been thrust headlong into a wonderful world of bureaucracy: Conveyance lawyers, letters of administration, contracts, agents, knowledge about taxes. Off and on, I find myself feeling like a child. Like these are matters I should have knowledge about, but don't. In these moments, I realise how sneaky Singapore is, how its culture of uniformity finds its way into one's flesh, embodies itself in the ways we think. Surely, there is no one way to be an adult. When I left you, I learned to eat three meals a day for under $5. I hacked the rental market, and survived. I found my own family, wrote about it, carved a career from loss. Surely, this is some sort of adulthood that deserves recognition.

One of the last things I find in your apartment, I find on the final day of clean-up: A bright orange noose made from plastic rope, measured and looped, placed together with illustrated measurements, pushed to the back of Gramps' bottom drawer. It has been carefully double-bagged, and as I unpack it, I expect to find some random purchase Gramps had made and forgotten about. Instead, I come upon this object – an intention so deliberately crafted, it causes all the hairs on the back of my neck to stand.

I know what I am looking at when I stumble upon it, but am unable to process it as real. My reflexive response is that I am having some sort of nervous breakdown. Finally, I think. All the feelings I thought I never had about my father hanging himself, are materialising in some sort of psychotic break.

It is only when I find the suicide note, written the year Nana died, unopened till now, that I understand the noose was never used – Gramps had kept it as a safety net.

Taking out the last of the garbage, I think to myself that maybe I have been wrong all these years, that maybe I did inherit some of this family's genetic traits. After all, there were many times in my life that I wanted to die. Many periods I had fantasised about it constantly. It was not a dramatic desire that announced its presence in loud sobs or melodramatic love songs. It grew slowly, quietly. A strong wanting for the inevitable to come quickly – tiredness the weight of bricks. These thoughts were the most prevalent the years I was living hand-to-mouth, waiting every other month for the power to be cut, moving house repeatedly because rents had doubled or leases were over or landlords just did not want me there anymore.

Did you ever feel that way – too tired with life to see it as more than anything but a chore? Those feelings, they do not go away. But I have learned to master mine. To set them aside, acknowledge their presence, turn my back to their murmurings.

Did you ever read about the two young women who jumped from a flat in Toa Payoh? One was 21, the other 30. I read they were a couple. The news reached only the tabloids; they appropriated the tragedy as scandal, focusing on who had "gone to therapy", who had been "torn between boy and girl", how the younger woman had defied her parents.

What nobody wanted to talk about was the fact that their bodies were found clad in red – a message to anyone fluent in local Chinese superstition: If you died by suicide dressed in red, it meant that you intended to return for revenge.

Something else no one wanted to talk about: The red string tied around each of their fingers – a symbol of their desire to be together in the next life.

I remember weeping when I read the article, feeling oddly complicit, oddly guilty. What had we done as a society to these two women, that even their love for each other could not undo? I had not known either of them, but I saw myself in their deaths. I saw their bodies as mine, their rage as my own. I wept over the act but took strength in the message: This is not the last you will see of us.

A friend once told me that anger and disappointment were two sides of the same coin – she said that anger was disappointment in disguise. Anger is bigger, louder, a force that pushes outward. Disappointment runs deeper, closer to collapse, to the parts of us that are soft, vulnerable.

I have learned to hone my anger like a knife. I carry it around for self-defence. My anger at you, at this homophobic country, at leaders too self-important to really care about anything, much less us. My anger at how so many queer friends of mine, born less middle-class, less fair-skinned, more non-conforming, have had it even worse, thrust into the world with even less luck to weaponise.

I am not sure why I bring all this up now. Why I am talking to walls. Why I am talking to you, the ghost of the woman I hated so much that the first thing I said when I heard she was dying was: "Good. I hope it is slow, and I hope it hurts."

Those words, so final. Not just for you, but also for me: Is this really what I have become?

Perhaps this rage needs to die with you. No point, after all, stabbing at air. And shouldn't I be happy coming back to this apartment, this windfall that solves all the problems caused by my leaving it?

I should be glad that you no longer haunt me, that your spectre exists only in photographs, in the minds of your few remaining friends. I should be glad that all you are is ash.

There is just one problem with letting the anger go – what to do with all that remains.

What of this disappointment settling in my bones? This house that failed at becoming home. These cracked tiles, this peeling paint, the wind whistling through windows.

What of this disappointment? These clothes left out to dry. This unfinished book. That broken lamp. This child you leave behind.

Tania De Rozario is a writer, visual artist, and the author of *Tender Delirium* (Math Paper Press, 2013) and *And the Walls Come Crumbling Down* (Math Paper Press, 2016 /Gaudy Boy, 2020). She was the 2020 winner of the *New Ohio Review*'s Nonfiction Contest and the 2011 winner of the Golden Point Award for English Poetry. Her poetry, prose and comics can be found in journals, including *The Malahat Review, Sow's Ear Poetry Review, Prairie Schooner Online Journal, Blue Lyra Review, Margin – The Asian American Writers Workshop Journal, carte blanche, Softblow* and *subTerrain Magazine*, among others.

OTHER BOOKS IN THE SERIES

FEATURING CONTRIBUTIONS BY
Anitha Devi Pillai, Anthony Goh, P N Balji,
Bernard Harrison, Chris Henson, Christopher Ng,
Clement Mesanas, Daniel Yap, Darren Soh, Dinesh Rai,
Fong Hoe Fang, Gilbert Koh, Kenny Chan, Lester Kok,
Mark Laudi, Nizam Ismail, Olivier Ahmad Castaignede,
Roland Koh, Sanjay Kuttan, Vicky Chong

FEATURING CONTRIBUTIONS BY
Adlena Oh-Wong, Amy Poon, Ng Choong San,
Cynthia Chew, Dawn Lee, Dawn Sim, Janet Goh,
Jennifer Heng, Jenny Wee, Kalthum Ahmad,
Karen Tan, Landy Chua, Loretta Urquhart,
Paige Parker, Petrina Kow, Sangeeta Mulchand,
Shaan Moledina-Lim, Chiong Xiao Ting,
Lin Xiuzhen, Yen Chua and Zalina Gazali

FEATURING CONTRIBUTIONS BY
Margaret Thomas, Sadie-Jane Alexis Nunis, Christina Thé, Louis Tong, Alvin Tan, David Kwee, Hoh Chung Shih, Wong Ting Hway, Chee Soo Lian, Natalie Ng, Charmaine Leung, Crispin Rodrigues, Jacintha Abisheganaden, Kelvin Tan, Usha Pillai, Andrew Koh, Patrick Sagaram, Loh Guan Liang, Sarah Voon, Koh Jee Leong